MANAGER'S GUIDE TO

Unleashing the Intrapreneur

Debbie Wooldridge

ttcInnovations
3281 Avenida De Sueno
Carlsbad, CA 92009
www.ttcInnovations.com

Ordering Information:
Quantity sales. Special discounts are available on quantity purchases by corporations, associations, and others. For details, contact the "Special Sales Department" at the address above.

Manager's Guide to Unleashing the Intrapreneur/
Debbie Wooldridge. —1st ed.
ISBN 978-0-9981075-1-6

Contents

i

To the managers of Millennials who understand that legacy matters and only survives with trust and passing the torch.

Acknowledgments

I would like to thank my wonderful husband, Chris, and my amazing Millennial children, Doug and Jessica, as well as their fabulous spouses, Emily and Collin — all of whom have tirelessly supported me throughout this dream. Special thanks to Emily Wooldridge for serving as my editor. I also want to thank all our talented team at ttcInnovations for the creative and inspiring work they do every day to help companies successfully train managers to support Millennials effectively as they join their organizations.

If the highest aim of a captain were to preserve his ship, he would keep it in port forever.

— Saint Thomas Aquinas

Introduction

This book reveals the most important resource your company could ever secure and a pathway toward procuring that valuable commodity. What is it that is so priceless yet attainable for all businesses and organizations, no matter their field, commodity being sold, or services being rendered? An empowered and equipped team that can produce productivity with positivity. So then, how do we create passion within our teams? That's just it — *we* don't create the actual passion; rather, we create an environment conducive for a team to thrive within.

By working with the company leadership, Human Resource team, and your department to recognize what the team needs to thrive and what needs to be implemented, your whole team will develop strategies and methods to create that amazing environment. Within that new workspace, the company will unearth a hidden treasure. What could that be? Millennials! The purpose of this book is to create a healthy environment where passion and innovation is evident, and especially so for Millennials.

Within 10 years, Millennials (born between 1980 and 2000) are expected to comprise a whopping 75% of the workforce. Millennials are taking over, and the survival of your company depends on attracting and retaining top Millennial talent. How do you do this? Tap into their intrapreneurial spirit!

Sit back and read this story. Then ask yourself, which manager am I? Be honest!

A Tale of Two Managers

Wendy had been working in the IT department at a local real estate co-op since right after college. Not even two years after her college graduation, she routinely attended monthly strategy sessions with the real estate agents, brokers, and administrative team members. In August during a meeting, Ron, one of the agents, ran in about 20 minutes late complaining that he had to run over to the hardware store to get a key made because he had a couple different showings scheduled for one of his listings and he had the only key. Several other agents in the room immediately sympathized with Ron, each of them sharing how many lunches or meetings they had missed and even potential showings they had to cancel because they couldn't get a key!

Wendy was puzzled by this. "Don't all houses have lockboxes?" she wondered. "Why would you need an extra key?"

The agents quickly explained that many home sellers prefer appointment-only viewings. Additionally, some listing agents want to be present when potential buyers are viewing a house so that they can answer questions, give a history of the house, and gauge reactions to the viewing. So, bottom line — no, lockboxes are not always available, which sadly often means a last-minute dash over to the hardware store to get a spare key made so that the home can be shown.

After the meeting, Wendy went back to her cubicle, still contemplating this dilemma. Surely in today's world there had to be a better way! Then it hit her — what if she could create a smartphone application to duplicate the key securely and send the file to a designated approved recipient, who could then use that file to have a key made themselves? No more need for the agent to do all the running around!

Wendy shared this idea with her manager, Tom. Tom immediately shut her down, telling her that wasn't her job! She needed to be working on the monthly system updates. That was what the company needed from her, not a system to solve a problem so that the agents could eat lunch! Wendy went back to the system updates, but her mind kept spinning around this idea. During a break later in the week, she had a chance to talk with a couple of the agents. She shared her idea for a way to securely copy and distribute keys. They loved the idea and immediately encouraged her to make it happen! Unfortunately, Tom was still not on board, even after one of the agents approached him to explain how helpful this would be to all the agents.

Fast forward two and a half months, and Tom was still only focused on monthly updates to the computer system when Wendy walked in and handed in her resignation.

Within a month, Wendy began working in the IT department of the co-op's biggest competitor. She approached her manager, Letitia, with the issues the agents had shared and her concept to create a secured solution. Letitia was excited! She immediately scheduled a meeting for Wendy to share her idea with the executive team. Within one month, funding was approved and a team was assigned to work with Wendy. A prototype was built and tested. Success! The marketing department was brought on and within 18 months, InstantAccess was on the market.

What happened at the real estate co-op? Tom is no longer managing the IT department, and the co-op is now paying a monthly fee to use the InstantAccess secured key distribution application proudly developed by Wendy and her team at the competitor's real estate agency! Oh, what could have been!

Which kind of manager are you? Are you Tom or Letitia? Do you feel this story is far-fetched? Absolutely not — Millennial intrapreneurs are among us! Their ideas, intuition, and intelligence is around us, but it is incredibly underutilized and goes unnoticed — or even worse — unsupported! It's our job to attract and support Millennials so that our companies can reap the benefits of this innovative and creative asset!

You may be thinking that Millennials don't want to work for companies — they want to be their own bosses. Well, here's the truth about that — discovered by a study of more than 1,500 Millennials (ttcInnovations, 2016).

1500 MILLENNIALS INTERVIEWED
by ttcInnovations 2016

ARE MILLENNIALS ENTREPRENUERS?

6%
Working as Entrepreneur

70%
Working PT or FT with Company

{ Are Millennials incapable?
Are they not trying?
NO AND NO. }

The odds are against them.

THESE ODDS CAN CHANGE IN THEIR FAVOR.

We have the power to redirect that entrepreneurial spirit into the company instead of losing great employees.

This Millennial workforce is filled with the spirit of entrepreneurism. "But if Millennials have such an entrepreneurial spirit, why aren't they opening their own businesses?" you might wonder. One of the biggest reasons that they don't is one of the biggest opportunities for you and your company! It's risk avoidance.

Millennials simply don't have the financial wherewithal to take on the risk of starting a new venture all on their own without the stability of an established staff and infrastructure. Most Millennials have a high debt-to-income ratio that makes them very unappealing candidates for financial backing from banks for startup funds.

Okay, now that you are aware of this untapped potential at your disposal, how do you tap in? Millennials are quickly realizing there are companies that offer the unique opportunity to drive change from within the organization using company funds and infrastructure to support the effort. Millennials are looking for companies that help them embrace their entrepreneurial spirit in an intrapreneurial world.

Intrapreneurialism is a win-win situation for Millennials and you! You and your company reap the benefits of enthusiastic, innovative, and committed employees while the Millennials enjoy the opportunity to embody an entrepreneur within the safe confines of an established enterprise. This reciprocal nature is the key to a happy and healthy work environment for the majority of the future workforce. Get ahead of this transition by changing today.

Initializing Intrapreneurialism

So, what exactly is an intrapreneur and how do companies benefit from creating environments that encourage employees to become one? Intrapreneurs are the gainfully employed workers of successful companies that use the staff, infrastructure, and resources of their company as catalysts to foster, forge, and bring to market new products or processes.

Because there is already sound foundation beneath, these innovators, once they make the decision to move in the intrapreneurial direction, have the ability to bring change without incurring the typical risks of being an entrepreneur like failing before beginning, losing funding, or even going belly up. Unlike entrepreneurs, intrapreneurs have the resources and capabilities of the company at their disposal to help them take an idea and make it into a reality.

Conceptually, the term intrapreneur is not new, but the climate in which they must operate is. At the beginning of this movement in 1978, U.S. management consultants Gifford and Elisabeth Pinchot first used this word in a research paper. In 1985, Gifford Pinchot authored a book entitled "Intrapreneuring." Steve Jobs was also quoted a few years later using the term intrapreneurship in a September 30, 1985 *Newsweek* interview, where he stated, "The Macintosh team was what is commonly known as intrapreneurship-only a few years before the term was coined — a group of people going in essence back to the garage, but in a large company." These intrapreneurs paved the way for generations to come and demonstrated how to reach success despite a rough landscape.

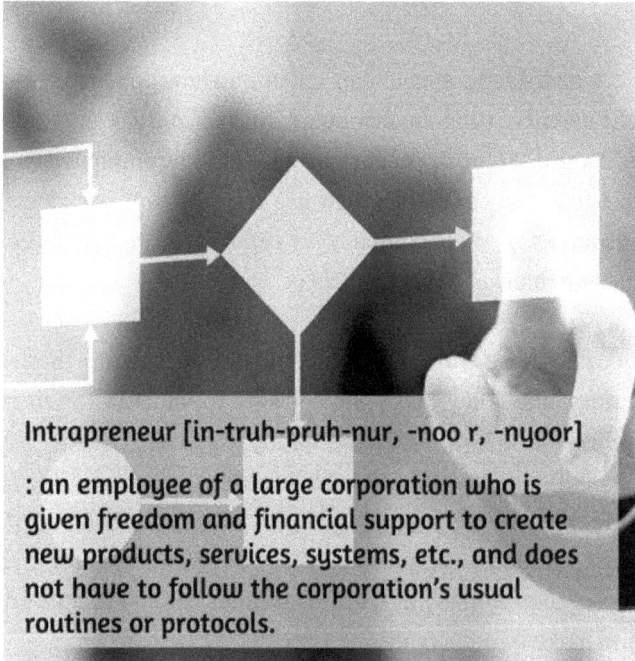

Intrapreneur [in-truh-pruh-nur, -noo r, -nyoor]

: an employee of a large corporation who is given freedom and financial support to create new products, services, systems, etc., and does not have to follow the corporation's usual routines or protocols.

The *American Heritage Dictionary of the English Language* defines intrapreneur as "a person within a large corporation who takes direct responsibility for turning an idea into a profitable finished product through assertive risk-taking and innovation." Notice how this definition does not state that intrapreneurs are just the executives at the top. Rather, all the levels of the ladder are more than capable of becoming intrapreneurial in their approach to their positions.

Steve Jobs was the ultimate innovator. No one can argue with this, and those who came after him and embodied his inquisitive, intellectual spirit are intrapreneurs because of these traits. These workers translate their innovation into reinventing and refining company products and processes without compromising what has already been built.

Intrapreneurs have the freedom and autonomy for professional growth while provided with the support needed to continue innovating, experimenting with, and seeking new products, policies, technologies, and applications that will help increase a company's productivity. Additionally, intrapreneurs have the unique talent of being able to recognize and solve important problems that may be holding the company back from reaching its fullest potential.

Not all employees have realized their intrapreneurial drive and put it into gear. Being an intrapreneur requires employees to push assertively against the status quo of the company, embrace change, work extra hours and in many instances, forgo full recognition and credit for their work and ideas. For those who do harness their power, the payoffs can be huge both to the company and the intrapreneur. Every employee has the potential to become an intrapreneur, but not all managers encourage or allow this spirit to flourish.

In some cases, the intrapreneurial drive of Millennials has been redirected by companies that have stopped short of fully embracing their spirit. These companies have become confined within a culture of 'this is the way it's always been done.' The fear of failing or legitimately lacking the resources to fully support ideas drives the status quo. How can you and your company break free and form a new, brighter future?

The risk of losing relevancy within the marketplace has reached a critical all-time high. Making this shift from the top down and bottom up will require everyone in the company totem pole to enter into a work environment that is conducive to change. This safe environment is where new thinking derives from taking chances. **Everyone** has to make the shift for this to work.

The imminent reality is that managers and companies that do not find ways to embrace the intrapreneurial spirit will fall behind and their market share will suffer greatly, resulting in the loss of opportunity to create intrapreneurs and attract new recruits. According to the 2016 Deloitte Millennial Survey Winning Over the Next Generation of Leaders (Deloitte, 2016), only 16 percent of Millennials see themselves with their current employer a decade from now. This absence of company loyalty is a serious challenge for any manager, as Millennials represent the largest segment of the workforce in the United States at this time.

Millennials desire to be autonomous, be creative, and live meaningful lives. But because current company landscapes impede on that, their careers are driven elsewhere, to companies that support their priorities. Companies that welcome and provide

Millennials with intrapreneurial opportunities entice employees to stay and help the company move forward. Millennials will dedicate futures to companies that stake their confidence in and allocate resources to them. The future of corporate America belongs to the individuals and the companies that embrace the idea of the intrapreneur.

This book is about establishing and promoting intrapreneurship in your organization to help generate new business growth, support and sustain innovation, as well as accelerate and manage change as the workplace adapts to address the needs and desires of Millennial employees. If you're wondering if this is possible, don't worry — it is! This book will provide you with examples of intrapreneurial supporting superstars like 3M, Edward Jones, and PwC, which have already successfully implemented the practices discussed in this book. We'll show you their journey toward success.

These companies have a few things in common. First, they have already recognized that Millennials are a different generation who have very different needs. Second, they have taken steps to make real changes in their organizations to attract and retain Millennials. These companies are succeeding because they make the most of the Millennials within and attract more to join the team! This has been validated, as these companies have been recognized on *Fortune Magazine's* "100 Best Workplaces for Millennials" (*Fortune Magazine*, 2016).

Each of the companies included in this book were interviewed as a part of a podcast series, The Millennial Career Playbook podcast, available on www.tmcpb.com (Debbie Wooldridge and

Hy Bender, 2016). These companies share their experiences and the successful outcomes that have resulted from implementing Millennial-friendly practices. Links out to the full podcast interview for each company mentioned are included so you can hear each interview in its entirety.

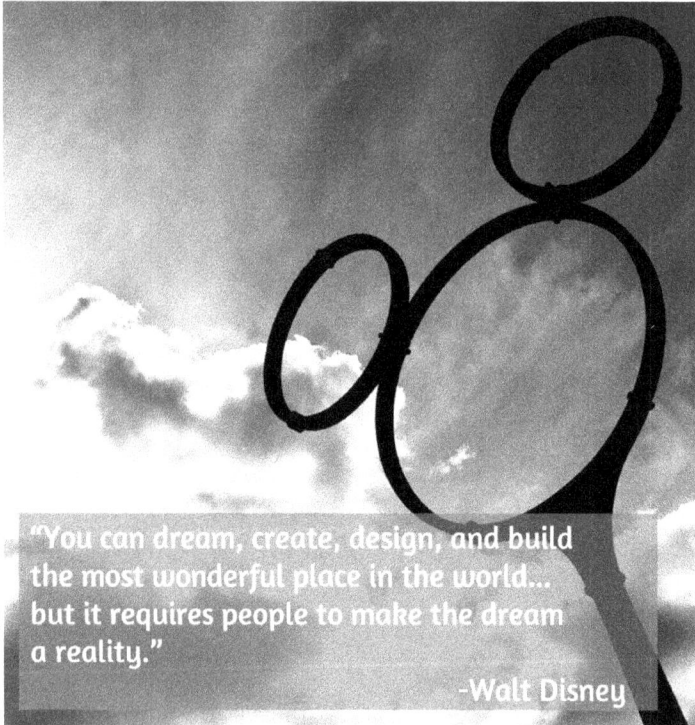

"You can dream, create, design, and build the most wonderful place in the world... but it requires people to make the dream a reality."

-Walt Disney

Part I: Creating an Attractive Environment

CHAPTER 1

Creating a Culture

Savvy managers know that innovation and out-of-the-box thinking are critical to keeping their department strong and relevant in today's rapidly changing corporate environment. Knowing it and implementing it are two very different things, though! Innovation requires innovators. Recognizing these innovators, these intrapreneurs, is essential to your company's success. Remember what Walt Disney taught us — it's the people that make everything happen.

Large and small companies alike are being challenged in today's corporate environment to survive and grow by finding cost effective ways to harness the ideas of their employees. Let's look at a couple situations where this is evident.

Becoming Obsolete

In 1985, David Cook founded perhaps the most well-known video rental empire, Blockbuster. From the start, David's business model was to rent videos at a fixed price per video in a brick-and-mortar store. By 1999, the company was valued at over 2.5 billion. And, by 2004, the franchise reached its peak with more than 9,000 stores.

So, what happened? In 2000, John Antioco, the CEO of Blockbuster, was presented with an opportunity to buy a relative newcomer to the home movie viewing business — Netflix — for a mere $50 million. John passed on the deal because he thought monthly subscription services for unlimited movie rentals was a small-niche business. Today, Netflix's market capitalization is over $50 billion. And what about Blockbuster? The final store shut its doors in early 2014. The billions that could have been! And the 9,000 buildings and their employees and patronage? All gone!

If only John would have had an intrapreneur advising him! The steadfast decision to operate business as usual and the resistance to change was the undoing of the Blockbuster empire. Now let's flip the scenario and see what happens when you have the wherewithal and winning intrapreneurial spirit.

Ascending to Dominance

The summer of 1991 was likely the lowest point in the early history of Sony's involvement in the emerging world of video gaming. It was Friday afternoon at the start of annual Consumer Electronics Show in Chicago where Sony announced its partnership with Nintendo to build a "Play Station". The intention was to build an add-on that would support the play of both game cartridges and compact discs. This would revolutionize the gaming industry by creating a multi-functional game console. The next day, Nintendo publically announced at the same convention that they were in discussions with the Dutch electronics company Philips N.V. (a major global competitor of Sony in televisions, radios, compact discs and more) to build a different compact disc reading add-on for their Super NES.

This announcement was confusing to the public and created much frustration for then Sony President Norio Ohga. How did he respond? He quickly appointed an intrapreneur, Ken Kutaragi to head a project to design a complete game console that would be entirely Sony's property.

By December 1994, Sony released the first widely available PlayStation console. This was followed a couple years later with the release of the PlayStation 2 (PS2). PS2 toppled the entire video gaming industry and tilted everything in Sony's favor through the first few years of the 21st century. Today, Sony remains in the forefront of gaming supremacy.

What if Ohga had walked away after the embarrassment of the Nintendo announcements? Sony gaming would have likely gone the way of Blockbuster!

Today's companies that fail to embrace innovation may well become the next Blockbuster, Borders, or Circuit City. But those that cultivate a culture that embraces the intrapreneur will likely enjoy the successes of Sony, Google, Facebook, Apple, and Microsoft.

Incorporating intrapreneurs into a company makes sense when you look at these different companies. This ability to capture the innovative attitudes of intrapreneurs within your company to help ensure growth seems intuitive.

Embracing the spirit of intrapreneurialism can be both enjoyable and profitable for your employees, and you as a manager, particularly if you consider yourself intrapreneurial by interest, discipline, personality, and skill set. However, theorizing on how this could help your company grow and ensure continued success is much easier than actually implementing.

Companies are built on structure and hierarchies that have been built to establish operational processes. These processes have led the company to its current level of success. So, when you introduce the idea of innovation and intrapreneurialism into the equation, it is often met with concerns about the true benefits that will result from a change in the status quo. It's difficult to forecast the immediate benefits of intrapreneurs and therefore, challenging to convenience others that this is a needed change.

Although it can be difficult to convince others of the need to create a culture of intrapreneurialism, you are not alone in your desire to make it happen within your department. A study conducted in conjunction with American Express found that 58% of managers are either very willing or extremely willing to support Millennials who want to be intrapreneurs in their company (Millennial Branding, 2012).

How do you know if your company is ready to become more intrapreneurial? Evaluate the list of characteristics of an intrapreneurial company below and then determine how closely your company culture currently matches these.

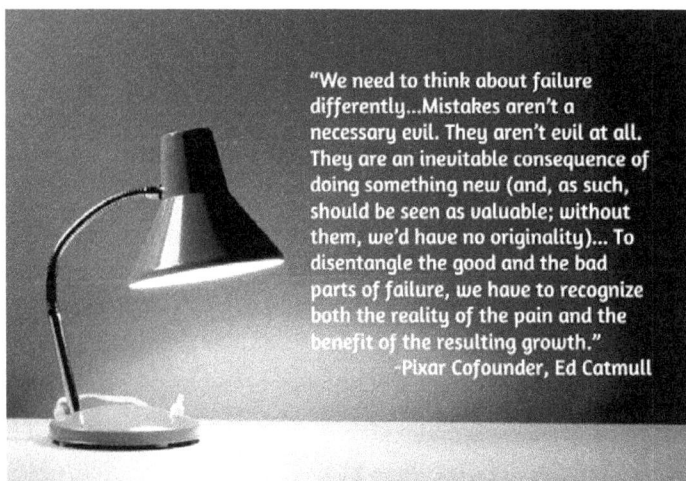

"We need to think about failure differently...Mistakes aren't a necessary evil. They aren't evil at all. They are an inevitable consequence of doing something new (and, as such, should be seen as valuable; without them, we'd have no originality)... To disentangle the good and the bad parts of failure, we have to recognize both the reality of the pain and the benefit of the resulting growth."
                                    -Pixar Cofounder, Ed Catmull

Characteristic #1: Willing to take risks — Companies that take the calculated risk time and again and plunge into promising markets or products often receive rewards such as an ever-increasing share price and market dominance. Not all innovations will be successful. Companies that embrace an intrapreneurial spirit have developed a "safety net" for innovative employees to reduce their personal risk to an acceptable level. Failure is recognized as the first step to success.

Characteristic #2: Embracing flat structure versus hierarchical — There is a significant difference in the way an intrapreneurial organization operates compared with a typical corporate hierarchical power structure. Intrapreneurial organizations operate within a flatter structure. Emphasis is placed on networking, teamwork, and the shared sacrifice, not title or tenor.

Characteristic #3: Eliminating road blocks — An intrapreneurial organization cuts out the so-called red tape in order to skillfully move new products, processes, or services through the organization.

Characteristic #4: Keeping an open mind — Managers in an intrapreneurial company solicit the opinions and ideas of their employees. There's not one manager who is so knowledgeable that he or she can afford to ignore the promising ideas of the team whenever they might arise.

Characteristic #5: Identifying intrapreneurs — The innovative manager is constantly looking to identify the intrapreneurs within their team and actively working to encourage budding intrapreneurs to flourish. Employees that possess this quality are almost always present in companies that embrace the intrapreneurial spirit. Virtually everyone has some internal creativity waiting to be expressed. Empowering these individuals by offering opportunities to express their creativity is one of the easiest ways to expand innovation in your department.

Characteristic #6: Encouraging transparency — Employees are entrusted with important company information and included in department decision making. No shut-door meetings. Team members are asked for feedback about the disseminated information. Employees feel involved in the overall day-to-day business process of their department regardless of their individual role. They are expected to do their assigned tasks, but also to chime in should they have contributions to their departments or others.

Characteristic #7: Rewarding proactivity — Managers avoid trying to control every aspect and detail of activity happening in their department. Instead, managers are "hands-off," rewarding individual team members who rise to the challenge, take charge, and find ways to help the department exceed business goals. Managers are active team members too, with the same expectations for themselves as their team — expected to contribute in big team projects, but not intrude in the day-to-day tasks of the team.

Characteristic #8: Empowering decision making — Managers give each person the green light to make decisions that have an impact on the work they do. Team members are held accountable for what happens next.

Characteristic #9: Encouraging engagement — Managers allow intrapreneurs to engage others and create excitement around their ideas.

Characteristic #10: Providing ownership — Managers allow each person on the team to feel ownership over the department. Ownership encourages intrapreneurs to be willing to contribute to the overall success of the team.

Characteristic #11: Fixing problems as they occur and avoiding procrastination — Managers take responsibility for issues and work to address them right away. Failure to do so may cause the problem to escalate and derail the intrapreneur's ability to innovate.

Characteristic #12: Supporting healthy competition — Opportunities are provided for the intrapreneurs on the team to have a sense of healthy competition. However, team members are aware that their success is intertwined and interdependent.

"Company culture is the product of a company's values, expectations and environment."
    - Courtney Chapman

So do you feel that your company matches the majority of these characteristics? What about your own department? Are you ready to introduce a culture of intrapreneurialism in your department and help ensure your company remains relevant, profitable, and growing?

You can be the beginning of the movement within your company. You can take the lead! All it takes is for you to be willing to make a change within your department. In essence, you have to be willing to be an intrapreneur yourself! Here are a few tips you should be following as you begin to create an intrapreneurial culture in your department:

Tip #1: Be intentional with your vision. Clearly define the vision that your department will operate under moving forward. Ensure that your vision aligns with the intrapreneurial characteristics mentioned earlier.

Tip #2: Create a plan that designates unstructured time. Innovation needs time to develop. Make a plan for how intrapreneurs will be afforded the time to experiment with new ideas without being penalized or expected to do so on their own personal time. Remember the realtors having to use their lunch or meeting times to make keys — they were using both personal and professional time!

Tip #3: Step in and step back. Give just enough structure and support to help intrapreneurs navigate uncertainty and tap into the creative process without stifling it. Strike a balance — ask your team to hold you accountable.

Tip #4: Identify meaningful measurements. Determine what measurements will be used to evaluate the effectiveness of the innovation.

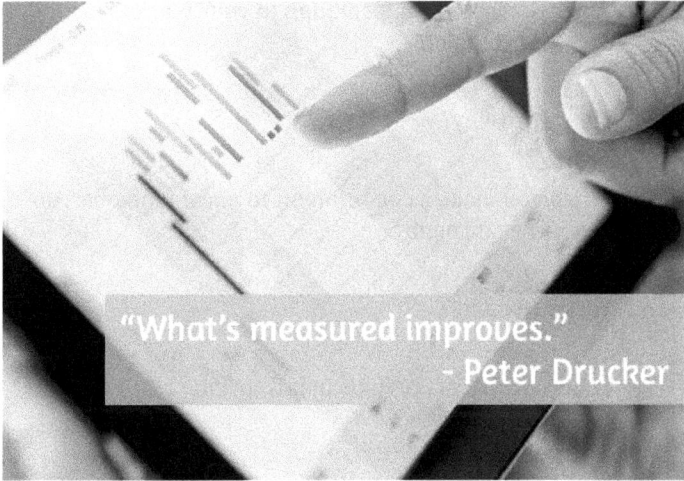

"What's measured improves."
- Peter Drucker

Tip #5: Recognize success. Don't wait for an annual Innovation Award to reward your team. The most powerful and robust type of recognition—the kind that shapes organizational values—often occurs more informally. Establish a program that allows opportunities to regularly call out individual success.

Following these tips can help you to encourage growth, innovation and ingenuity within your team. But, before you can implement this change into your work culture, you will need to determine your own readiness for change.

Activity — Evaluating Cultural Change Readiness

Instructions: Use the questions below to help evaluate your readiness to embrace intrapreneurs in your department:

1. When you convey information to your team, is it sincere and complete?

   Yes or **No; why?**

2. When you make a commitment to a team member, do you follow through?

   Yes or **No; why?**

3. Is the success of creating an intrapreneur culture a top priority for you?

   Yes or **No; why?**

4. Do you have adequate resources to begin to implement this change?

   Yes or **No; why?**

5. Is there a shared understanding for the need for the change within your department?

   Yes or **No; why?**

> 6. Do you have approval to begin to implement this change from senior management?
>
> **Yes or No; why?**
>
> 7. Are you 100% vested in supporting this change within your department even if immediate positive results are not experienced?
>
> **Yes or No; why?**
>
> Be honest. Remember knowing and doing are two different things.
>
> By now, you have read that you *should* be doing these things. However, we are not taking inventory of what you *plan* to do, but rather, what you've done up until now.
>
> If the answers to any of these questions are currently no, evaluate what groundwork still needs to be completed to begin to implement this change in your department.

Once you have determined you are ready to lead this shift in culture, you can then begin to empower your team to innovate by giving those tools, time, resources, and support. This intrapreneurial culture results in greater commitment of team members and better products and services to sell.

Changing Work Culture Begins with YOU

Still doubting that a change in culture will really make a difference in your company? You'll doubt no further when you look at what Anne Donovan has learned from her accomplished work. Anne works within the Human Capital department of one of the world's largest professional services networks, PricewaterhouseCoopers (PwC). She co-authored *"NextGen,"* the largest (44,000 people) generational study in history to definitively uncover the barriers to changing the current business model.

The results of this groundbreaking study demonstrated to Donovan and her team that companies are currently primarily managed by Gen Xers (born between 1965 and 1979) and have a common denominator — an attitude that revolves around themselves: "I'm controlling my world, so I like my world. If I'm learning, developing, and getting paid, then I am happy at work." Gen Xers can sometimes be control freaks.

In stark contrast, Donovan states, "Millennials have a shared mentality that is centered on how their team works together, how much support and appreciation they feel, and whether they have enough flexibility to [enjoy] a full life."

Bridging the gap between those worldviews is challenging, but doable...as evidenced by PwC's roughly 180,000 global employees now being over 75% Millennials. And, addressing these issues head on and adapting the company culture isn't just happening at PwC.

Donovan underscored this incredible shift by sharing her findings: "We have had conversations with clients and let me just tell you that the number of client requests I've received in the last 12 months has heated up significantly. I'm spending quite a bit of time in front of clients, because they now are saying, 'Wow, we have an issue with our staff. We don't know what it is, but we think it's Millennial related. We know PwC — you faced this already and you have thoughts about it.' It's very fun to see this evolution. I would bet my paycheck on the fact that every single company out there in every single country out there (because I'm also seeing it around the world with PwC) is going to have to get on this train if [they're] doing any hiring these days, because the lower levels [are] Millennials."

To listen to the entire interview with Anne Donovan, visit **The Millennial Career Playbook** website:

http://www.tmcpb.com/company-interviews/pricewaterhousecoopers/

(Donovan, 2015)

CHAPTER 2

Identifying Intrapreneurs

I nnovation and out-of-the-box thinking isn't every employee's first inclination, so it is important as a manager to recognize and support those who already want to innovate, and to foster creativity within those who don't. Ultimately, it is important to reconcile with the fact that some employees are very valuable but, even with the right coaching, may never gravitate toward intrapreneurialism.

Distinguishing Employees and Intrapreneurs

Intrapreneurs are members on your team who possess an entrepreneurial mindset. They are willing to take complete ownership of their assignments and responsibilities within the team. Employees, on the other hand, are engaged to do specific tasks and duties for a specific role within the team. This doesn't necessarily mean that employees are *just* on the assembly line, in their cubicle, or behind their computer screen and don't ever do anything outside of their daily duties. But it does mean that employees *just need* direction.

When hiring, most managers do not specify whether they want an employee or an intrapreneur at the outset. Generally, they are looking for someone with the minimum skill set necessary to fill an existing position. However, who you end up hiring can make a big difference on your team and can yield maximum results.

Employee — If you hire an employee, generally what you will see is a person who fulfills the duties of the job description. Employees tend to focus on succeeding at their current position within the company rather than on the overall success of the company or their upward advancement. Employees can be quick to run off when a higher paying job comes along due to a focus on what is presented at the time of hire, versus visualizing opportunities that may occur down the road.

Intrapreneurs — If you hire an intrapreneur, generally what you will see is a person who creates a wider and more robust job description for him or herself. They really embrace the caveat at the end of the job description that usually reads "other duties as assigned," and assign duties to themselves! Intrapreneurs focus on looking for ways to grow the company and advance their career with leadership experiences rather than just fulfilling the duties presented and getting paid. Intrapreneurs generally stay with a company to help grow the business, therefore making it possible to earn a higher salary as the company's profits increase. Intrapreneurs see the whole picture and know that as the scales tip, their fortunes do as well — their buy-in draws them further with the stakes high for all.

Selecting the Appropriate Candidates

Emily and Amy are both Millennial candidates applying for a sales associate position at a packaging company. Both have a business degree from the local university and both have had more than one year of real-life experience working in a sales-related position.

Both responded well to the typical interview questions. However, when each was asked what they would do to expand the market share over the next six months, their answers varied dramatically. Therein lies the difference within the initial interview process: open-ended questions having answers that are inspired by envisioning future success.

Emily responded that she would work closely with the head of sales to uncover what is working well so far by hearing her concerns, needs, and questions. She would observe with her fresh perspective, and then she would take that information and focus on strengthening those customer relations.

Amy's response was much different. Amy shared that she would start by looking at the top three packaging competitors to uncover what needs those companies are meeting that this company doesn't offer. She would then work with the company's product department to see what alternate solutions might be available to offer customers — whether it be looking at potential ways to offer new products, or repackaging existing products that more closely match what customers are looking for when going with a competitor.

Both candidates have solid plans for increasing market share and both would likely add value to the company's bottom line. Emily has potential to be a good sales employee, but Amy has the potential to be an intrapreneur! Both have skill sets that have been enhanced by their studies and experiences, but each has their own inclinations that come directly from their different paradigms.

So, which prospective is the better hire? I guess the answer to that question lies in your goal as a manager. If you are looking to help grow yourself, your department, and your company, hiring the intrapreneur makes the most sense! But if you have intrapreneurial members already on your team who need help to heed and implement their innovative plans, then hiring the employee could be the better option!

Having employees with an intrapreneurial spirit on your team is a good strategy to have moving forward. By employing this strategy, you ensure that your department is set up to be innovative and forward-thinking. To utilize this approach successfully, you need to look both internally (You may very well have a great group of intrapreneurs just waiting for the opportunity to innovate on your team today!) and outside your organization for people who possess this spirit. What does it look like? The five characteristics below are a great start to help you identify the intrapreneurs for your team and thus have great leaders in the field who can orchestrate employees:

Characteristic #1: Mission-oriented — Intrapreneurs naturally possess a sense of mission. So, when looking out for innovative candidates, ensure they believe in your mission and have the ability to help you set goals that will successfully grow your department.

Characteristic #2: Enthusiastically passionate — Intrapreneurs have a passion for their career. They love the path they have chosen for themselves and work to continually fuel that passion by pushing themselves to be inspired, creative, and successful.

Characteristic #3: Freedom-seeking — Intrapreneurs are people with a genuine desire for freedom within their career. They seek opportunities that promote freedom of creativity, as well as flexibility within their environment to enable them to contribute their best to your department's efforts.

Characteristic #4: Thirst for knowledge — When searching for the right intrapreneurs to support your department, be on the lookout for those individuals who are true lifelong learners. Intrapreneurs are always looking into the future and learning about how they can continually improve.

Characteristic #5: Visionary — Look for candidates who come to you with a vision for your department. When interviewing, intrapreneurs will be prepared to share their new ideas for your department and your company.

"The future belongs to those who see possibilities before they become obvious."
- John Scully

Activity — The Hunt for Intrapreneurs

Instructions: To target the right candidates to help integrate and inspire your team, begin by creating your ideal profile. Creating a candidate profile allows you to define a full, accurate picture of the ideal candidate. You'll understand the type of person you need in this position before you start interviewing, and you'll be able to tailor your interview questions and format to find the best qualities for the job.

When determining your candidate profile, keep in mind that you are specifically looking to add team members who demonstrate an intrapreneurial spirit. Create a profile that helps you identify candidates who share the values and goals of your department.

To begin this process, decide on the two to three most critical behavioral traits the ideal candidate will possess:

1.

2.

3.

Taking the time to develop a thorough candidate profile will help you attract and identify the best candidates. If you need to draft traits with bullet points, evaluate, review, and revise, then do it. This revision process allows you to cover all aspects of the ideal person.

Success Story — Inspiring Action

Finding great intrapreneurial candidates is definitely worth the time you invest in planning your recruitment process and successfully executing that plan. Lindsey Dole (Director of Human Resources at the blog-hosting giant, Tumblr) and her team recognize the importance of identifying the ideal candidates for their organization.

When looking for the ideal candidate to fill a role on a team at Tumblr, Lindsey shares just how the company invests time and effort into recruiting:

> "We look to see if the experience is relevant, and if the person has done that specific thing before or done something similar, or we feel like they can easily step into the tasks and the responsibilities that we're asking them to have."

> "I would also say in the interview, 'That's it,' glancing at a résumé and looking at the pieces of information that they use to apply. Then, when evaluating candidates either on the phone or in person, we will look for passion. We look for excitement. We look for people who want to work, not just in that particular job, but at Tumblr."

> "We oftentimes move people around in teams or change focuses based on the business needs. Having people who can stretch their wings and who do want to contribute in a lot of different areas, and are passionate about the company, and not just in that specific thing that they're being hired to do — that is really, really exciting when we come across that,

because it just helps us have a lot of confidence that that person is going to be not only a good fit now for the need that we're hiring for, but also in the future, as business needs develop."

Then once the intrapreneurs are hard at work at Tumblr, Lindsay shares how Millennials can be most successful by embracing the inviting environment where innovative ideas are not only anticipated and welcomed, but expected:

"Not being afraid to share your ideas. I think sometimes you can get used to [...] what you're doing..., or you can feel like there's not an avenue. I think if you really push through and share your ideas and speak up, [...] there's a lot that you can do. I think we look for our employees to take that initiative themselves. As I've mentioned earlier, we look for that in our applicants. If they're thinking outside the box and approaching their work from different ways and sharing their ideas, I think [they'll] have a really successful career. That usually comes with exposure to different things and opportunities coming."

"I would also say combining that with an appetite for really enjoying fast-paced environments, and being flexible. That will also allow for a lot of success. As I mentioned, we do shift teams and resources and things to align when business needs shift. I think adapting to that and learning to not be afraid of change or really truly embracing change as opportunity will lead to a lot of success, too. We look for that when we're hiring, as I mentioned, too. Just thinking about ways that they can contribute and offering to contribute in these areas. I think people with great ideas, thinking outside the box, being critical of things and having a general energy and enthusiasm for their work and the product that we work, that will lead to success."

Although Tumblr is a relatively young company, it is heavily used by Millennials. They have a clear goal to continue to grow the platform and have every capability to succeed because of a feasible and thought-out process for identifying and hiring intrapreneurs. By helping intrapreneurs push for new ways to share content on its platform, Tumblr will without a doubt continue increasing engagement and users.

To listen to the entire interview with Lindsey Dole, visit **The Millennial Career Playbook** website:

http://www.tmcpb.com/company-interviews/tumblr/

(Dole, 2015)

Part II: Establishing Engaging Experiences

CHAPTER 3

Anticipating Millennials' Aspirations

Establishing your company vision is just the first step. The second step is bringing the vision to fruition — setting goals. Identifying the characteristics of the Millennials that will help you achieve those goals is the third step, and it's a continuing journey. With your vision in sight, building your team isn't the end. Ensuring you've created a captivating and engaging work experience makes your team more attractive to intrapreneurs and increases retention rates as well. That's the journey — that's the ultimate goal. It is of no value to hire or select team members who possess the ability to innovate and drive your company forward if you do not offer an environment that encourages loyalty.

And, right now, many companies are failing dramatically at encouraging loyalty by not even scaling step one. According to the

2016 Deloitte Millennial study, two-thirds of Millennials expressed a desire to leave their organization by 2020. This is really a pretty disturbing statistic when you think about the effect on your company in terms of time and financial cost. This could constitute a financial burden from which your department or company might not be able to easily recover.

What is even more discouraging is that this situation is completely PREVENTABLE!

LOSING TALENT TAKES A TOLL $

$15K-$25K
Cost PER Millennial lost. Projected to increase in near future[1]

3-7 WEEKS
Time it takes for new employees to become productive[1]

2/3 WORKFORCE
Millennials who foresee leaving their current employer by 2020[1]

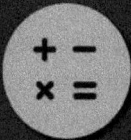

TOTAL COST
2/3 Millennial Workforce x $15K-$20K=hundreds of thousands of Preventable Expendtures[1]

60% WORKFORCE
Millennials who would be open to new opportunities RIGHT NOW[2]

DELOITTE, 2016 [1]
GALLUP, 2016 [2]

So is all hope lost? Do you just need to resign yourself to the fact that your department will need to dramatically increase the recruiting line item in your budget? No, not at all!

Real Recipes for Disaster: Failing Fast

Bob is the head recruiter at Massachusetts Manufacturing, a company with a legacy of producing aluminum storm windows for over 75 years. Bob has been diligently attempting to fill 15 open positions within the company, the majority of which are vacant because many of the company's Baby Boomers have entered retirement and existing employees haven't been promoted or moved within the company when appropriate to fill those spots.

While most of the open positions are within the production department, several of the job openings are management level. These positions have been open for months and Bob is getting a lot of negative feedback from department heads, whose productions are falling off due to reduced workforce. Bob has been told he needs to do whatever it takes to get these positions filled quickly or the company will begin losing customers due to delays in productivity. Basically, he has been instructed by the uppermost management to fill the empty seats with warm bodies.

Bob knows that the wages he is able to offer for the positions are definitely completive for the industry and, in general, higher than the median income of the community surrounding the manufacturing plant. Yet, he can't seem to get any applicants in the door. Bob has talked with several other Human Resource leaders in the community and is finding that most companies are not having the difficulties he is having in attracting applicants.

Bob knows that he is actually offering higher salaries and even better benefits than several of the other companies represented by these other HR leaders. So, what is the problem? Doesn't money matter anymore? Why aren't Millennials applying?

Which memo did Bob miss? What is he doing wrong? If you chuckled to yourself and said Bob should offer more money, then you are WRONG! Now, that isn't to say that Millennials aren't interested in money — they are. Like other generations, pay and financial benefits is the largest single factor that drives Millennials' choice of where to work. According to a survey of nearly 7,700 full-time employed Millennials (Deloitte, 2016), 22% did cite financial benefits as the number one driver for selecting a job. But this is actually less than a fourth of the entire group of survey respondents!

Even if your company is offering a relatively competitive financial package, money alone will not point Millennial intrapreneurs in the direction of your organization. What did the study uncover as the other key factors that Millennials look for when selecting a company?

Millennials' Must-Haves in Prospctive Employers

(Deloitte, 2016)

Category	Percentage
Innovation	6%
Professional Development	8.3%
Work Fulfillment	9.2%
Flexibility	11%
Upward Mobility	13.4%
Worklife Balance	16.8%

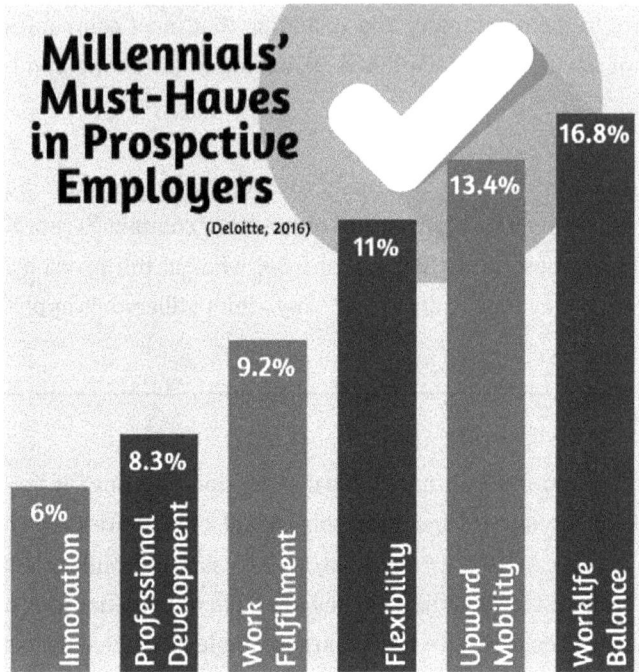

Offering a work environment that incorporates these other Millennial "must-haves" will help you will help you to be more successful than your competition in securing and retaining intrapreneurs.

"The people who make it to the top – whether they're musicians, or great chefs, or corporate honchos – are addicted to their calling ...they are the ones who'd be doing whatever it is they love, even if they weren't being paid"
- Quincy Jones

Activity — Measuring Your Appeal

Instructions: To determine what changes you need to make in your company's environment and thus attract and retain top intrapreneurial talent, you need to see how your organization measures up to the things that matter most to Millennials, as aforementioned. Review each of the statements below and then rank your company's current ability to support the factors most valued by Millennials.

	Strongly Disagree	Disagree	Agree	Strongly Agree
Offers work-life balance				
Provides opportunities to progress				
Offers flexibility				
Promotes professional development				
Offers mentoring				
Encourages an open-door policy				
Encourages innovation				
Provides positive impact on society				
Offers sense of purpose				

Remember, most Millennials choose organizations that share their personal values; it is never too late for you and your company to overcome areas that don't match up with these values. And this is the best place to start — with a clear direction in mind!

The remaining chapters in this section of the book will address each of these key motivators for intrapreneurialism and discuss strategies to plan, implement, and execute within your department and company. These strategies are designed specifically to increase your ratings in each of these areas and ensure you do not find yourself and your company in the same position as Bob from Massachusetts Manufacturing! Don't be like Bob — be so desirable that you have candidates beating down the door and teams that won't be leaving any time soon.

CHAPTER 4

Balancing Work and Life

O ne of the biggest distinguishers between Millennials and previous generations is that work does not define them. Family, friends, and making a difference in their community are much bigger drivers for this generation. They've collectively shifted their focuses; potential employers must also focus on striking a balance, too.

You are not inherently responsible for providing work-life balance for your team members, but proactively helping your team seek and maintain their own work balance is your responsibility. Fostering this balance will help you attract and retain the intrapreneurs you seek. Keep in mind that Millennials are most likely to be turned off by managers who offer a "that's the way it has always been done" rationale regarding workplace policies and procedures. Their status quo is to change the status quo with innovation and creativity.

"Employees who believe that management is concerned about them as a whole person – not just an employee – are more productive, more satisfied, more fulfilled.

Satisfied employees mean satisfied customers which leads to profitability."

– Anne M. Mulcahy

Living Life: Daily Grind or Getting into the Groove

Virginia and Peter both belong to a local chamber of commerce. After a few years of rubbing shoulders at meetings, they've struck up a friendship. Both are managers in charge of fairly large teams, working in companies from similar industries. They have often bounced work-related issues off each other during the networking events. They have come to rely on each other's professional opinions.

At the end of the most recent monthly meeting, Virginia mentioned to Peter that she wouldn't be at next month's event. He asked her what was going on. She replied, "Oh, my husband and I are taking a couple weeks off to go on a backpacking trip to Yosemite National Park." Peter looked surprised and said, "Two weeks? How can you possibly have time to take two weeks off? I could never take two weeks off to go backpacking!" Virginia looked at Peter and laughed, "Peter, you and I both have the same number of weeks of vacation in a year! You do have time to go backpacking or anywhere you could want to go!"

With a sigh, Peter replied, "That's easy for you to say. I never seem to have time. My work takes so much of my time. I'm at the office at 7:30, I leave around 6:30, and the weekends? Well, those are just the days available to catch up on all the work I didn't get done during the week because of meetings or other crises! You know what it's like, you have the same size team to manage that I do."

"Of course I know what it's like," Virginia said. "But what would happen tomorrow if you got sick? Who would do the work?"

"Sick? I don't have time to get sick!" exclaimed Peter. "But, I guess if I did, someone at the company would do the work I suppose."

"You know something, Peter, I used to be like you. I worked night and day, and even weekends. When I got home I was exhausted, but I would push myself and read my children a bedtime story. By the time I went to bed, I would be more than exhausted. The boss I had was very demanding. She was there early in the morning and didn't go home until late at night, and she always worked weekends. I felt I had to do the same. I needed the job to help support my family, just as you did. But then I changed companies."

"Of course, when I first started there, I continued to work the hours I had been working. But one day, the CEO of the new company came to my desk and passed me a card with a quote on it that said, 'What I do today is important because I will never have today again' — and then he left. I sat there stunned. I suddenly thought of what was important to me. While my work was important, I realized my children were more important."

"I also realized that personal time for myself was important. It was 4:30, the official closing time of the office. I straightened up my desk and felt a twinge of guilt about leaving, but I forced myself to leave. I was home by 5:00. My children and husband were surprised. I had a wonderful evening. It was not a chore to read a bedtime story that evening."

Peter was looking at his friend thoughtfully and then questioned Virginia about the work she had left on her desk. Virginia responded, "I never thought this to be possible, but I actually accomplished more the next day than I had in weeks."

"As I was leaving the next day, I stopped at my CEO's office and thanked him for the quotation. He told me a short story about advice his dad had given him many years ago when he first started the company and was working night and day. He referred to it as 'Balance of Life.' His dad told him to keep balance in his work, in his family life, and in time for himself. He explained to me that while all aspects of our life are important, without a balance, you become addicted and like all addictions — you eventually lose. He went on to tell me that who we are is NOT what we do to make a living. Who we are is a balance of our family, our work, and ourselves! It truly was the best advice I ever received."

Peter responded, "But I would never get my work done if I left at 4:30 at my company!" Virginia looked at Peter thoughtfully and said, "Well Peter, it may be the work environment that is the problem; give it a thought. If you have no balance with your work, you lose perspective and you actually lose focus on the important aspects of your job. Are you really at the right place for what you want out of your life?"

Many people go through life and get caught up in situations and circumstances that end up controlling them. Those who achieve balance have a defined plan centered on ensuring that all aspects of their lives are fulfilled.

How can you help your company ensure work-life balance is a priority? Below is a list of ways you should be helping your team achieve the goal of work-life balance:

Idea #1: Allowing remote work options — Consider allowing your team to work from home either regularly or on occasion (depending on the type of work to be completed). **Note:** The next chapter explains a variety of ways to make this concept work effectively in your environment.

Idea #2: Restricting hours worked — Many professions already do this for the sake of safety, such as pilots, air traffic controllers, and surgeons, as there have been many travesties that occurred when these types of workers were pushed to dangerous levels of exhaustion. Even if your industry doesn't have safety regulations, do you really want someone who is averaging two to three hours of sleep a night talking with your best customers? Do you think that their emotional state is steady enough to withstand whatever their sales day brings? What about your accountant — do you think their numbers will be accurate without functioning brain capacity? Consider creating a culture in which your team members are not expected to work after leaving their worksite. Discourage both the sending of and responding to email after hours. Encourage off-work time to be exactly that — OFF WORK! Asking that work devices be left at the office, powered off, or even only accessible on-site through the company server are all ways to approach this.

Idea #3: Promoting breaks through the work day — Taking a real break during the middle of the day can go a long way to keep stress and physical strain in check, not to mention emotional tension. Maybe nap time in kindergarten wasn't such a bad idea! People get cranky without proper rest and nourishment, just as young children do; but instead of throwing fits, adults lose stamina and patience. Ensure that your team takes a real break at lunch time and regular rest breaks. In many cases, this is enforceable by labor laws. Taking breaks throughout the day has actually been shown to increase productivity. Higher productivity means less need to work long hours and more fresh workers showing up each day!

Idea #4: Providing help for everyday tasks — Provide your team with opportunities for assistance with everyday tasks. This could be done in the form of on-site or near-site benefits that allow team members to get more of their personal or household responsibilities handled during work hours. Consider finding a local dry cleaning service that would be willing to come do on-site pickups and deliveries, auto repair or car washing services that would be willing to come on-site or provide concierge services. During the holidays, perhaps offer gift wrapping services, or even massage services on-site. There are so many opportunities! Discuss with your team which types of services would add the most value and then work together to make it happen. Often these businesses offer company discounts to obtain a volume of business, so it is a win-win for everyone!

Idea #5: Offering wellness opportunities — Having a healthier team can lead to less stress and far fewer absences, which can be a real boost to productivity. Provide opportunities either on-site or near-site for your team members to participate in a variety of wellness programs. Consider all options, including programs that support physical, emotional, and mental wellness for your team.

Idea #6: Watching for burnout — An important skill of a great manager is the ability to spot the beginnings of burnout. Chances are, your team member may not admit directly to you that he or she is feeling overworked or overwhelmed. Look for signs such as excessive absenteeism, increased errors, and physical exhaustion. If you spot any of these signs, step in! Talk with the team member to find out what he or she needs most right now to reduce the burnout. Is it time off, assistance on their current workload, or even reassigning some responsibilities? Make sure the team member knows that the goal is to provide support, not punishment — and that you are helping them to temporarily step away from a stressful situation, not step down.

Idea #7: Encouraging efficiency — Working more and being productive are not at all the same thing. In fact, often, the more hours your team member works, the less efficient he or she will become. Work with your team to evaluate your department's processes and procedures. Look for ways to create efficiencies in recurring tasks. "Work smart, not long." (Mental Health Foundation, 2016).

Idea #8: Encouraging vacation — Team members are often reluctant to take their earned days off, especially if they feel there is no one available to do their job while they are out. In an online survey of 1500 adults, 34% of employed Americans took no vacation days in 2016 (Skift, 2017). The ill effects of not taking vacation time are well documented and include fatigue, poor morale, health issues, and a reduction in productivity. Vacation time offers both mental and physical health benefits. It's vitally important as a manager to ensure that your team members actually take time off to recharge and unplug. Work with your team to create a plan that ensures workloads are covered and that all assignments can be completed while still allowing scheduled time off.

Idea #9: Sponsoring team and family events — Plan events that encourage team building, friendships among your department, and inclusion of family into work events. Include opportunities to take part in special community or local events. Charities, sports, and recreational activities such as bowling, movie nights, hay rides, or book clubs are all great ways to connect work and life together in a relaxed manner. One positive outcome is that team members who build extensive relationships with each other are much more likely to stay with the company as they become much more invested as a whole person.

Idea #10: Clarifying expectations — It's okay to expect team members to work long, hard hours during specific vital company operations. Perhaps you have quarterly reports that must be completed by the 10th business day of the month following a quarter end. Those nine days leading up to that cut-off may well require working late nights! But be mindful of the fact that team members cannot and should not be expected to sustain this extraordinary level of energy or hours as a constant work schedule. Team members will check out, burn out and/or leave if this is the norm. Commitment, engagement, productivity, and dedication do not equal 60- to 70-hour work weeks!

Idea #11: Allowing cross-over life needs into the workplace and vice versa — Keep an open mind that shopping at an online sale while sitting in the office at three in the afternoon is often mitigated by responding to a quick work call at 6:30 pm while the family is sitting down to dinner. The line between work time and life time is not likely as distinct as it was in previous generations. Trust that your team is making great choices and evaluate their effectiveness based on productivity — not by whether a personal issue is being taken care of during the work day or a work issue is being managed during family time.

Idea #12: Modeling the work-life balance you want to encourage — When you expect your team to attend a weekly conference call during your scheduled vacation, you are sending a powerful message to your team. Your actions set the tone for your team. You are telling the team that you expect each of them to be available 24/7. Make sure that you are demonstrating the importance of work-life balance instead of just talking about it. Your actions will override your words.

Activity — A Delicate Balancing Act

Instructions: Think about the opportunities you have to encourage work-life balance for your department and company. Use the following questions as a guide.

1. How might you have to adjust the way you each think about work-life balance?

2. What are some of the cultural norms that might need to shift to accommodate a more balanced working environment?

3. Identify the top three ways you currently support your team members' work-life balance. How do your team members make use of this support?

4. Meet with your team to identify the top concerns they have about work-life balance. Ask what THEY want and then make a plan to implement!

There are long-term benefits to encouraging your entire team to find a balance between their work and home lives. Take steps to ensure that your words, actions, and examples emphasize the need to have genuine satisfaction, inner peace, and balance. Team members that have the power to take control over their work and home lives can have a profound positive impact on their job satisfaction and performance, enabling you to do what is best and most effective for your company!

Success Story — Balancing in Action

Striking that perfect balance between career and family has always been a challenge for employees since the industrial revolution. However, this newest generation of workers are pushing companies to uphold the responsibility of making an environment that supports both spheres of life. Companies that gain a reputation for encouraging work-life balance are becoming increasingly attractive to Millennials and thus are more likely to draw a valuable pool of the best candidates for new job openings.

Ultimate Software, the leader in cloud-based personnel management software, is one such company. Laura Lee Gentry, Vice President of Talent, upholds this advantageous philosophy by putting the needs of Millennials at the forefront of strategic planning and implementing practices that do so.

"We were founded from day one with a people-first culture. Scott Scherr, our founder, has always believed that if you take excellent care of your people, that they will in turn take excellent care of your customers and everything else will sort itself out. That's a culture that a lot of companies talk about, but at Ultimate, they bring it to life in every single way in which they interact with their people, so that people-first culture is who we are at our center."

When asked about how this philosophy plays out for work-life balance, Laura Lee shares that the organization is centered and driven by a shared construct — harmony.

> "We refer to it as work-life harmony. We treat people like grownups that know what's expected of them. Our people work hard and they're very engaged. Everyone loves the company and wants it to be successful, so everyone does what it takes. We know people can't sustainably deliver if they aren't well-rested and healthy at home."

> "We have a team trip every year where we take all of our employees and their teams and their families on a trip. For example, this last weekend before Thanksgiving, the entire Development team and their families will go to Orlando for a two-and-a-half-day company-sponsored trip where you get to take your kids to either two days at Universal or Disney. My kids are thrilled, "You work for the coolest company in the world."

Additionally, Ultimate Software offers the opportunity for their employees to work remotely. Currently, about 40% of their employee base is virtual.

The company's culture of supporting a harmony between work and home life has really paid off. Ultimate Software consistently ranks at the top of the Fortune 100 Best Workplaces for Millennials. The 2017 ranking has Ultimate Software at number one!

To listen to the entire interview with Laura Lee Gentry,
visit **The Millennial Career Playbook** website:

http://www.tmcpb.com/company-interviews/ultimate-software/

(Gentry, 2015)

CHAPTER 5

Seizing Opportunities

Many Millennials believe they will likely change jobs every two to three years to get ahead in their careers (Deloitte, 2016). That is a lot of laying down roots and uprooting! Just like agriculture, the work culture is upset by the uprooting of team members. Losing the talent means that the next project outcomes will be less bountiful. Losing employees can be quite impactful to your team's morale and your company's bottom line. Finding ways to help the intrapreneurs on your team grow themselves and their careers can make all the difference in your company's successful future.

While most managers list managing people as their top priority, statistically, mid-level managers spend only three hours per week actually managing people and of that, only a very short two hours is actually spent coaching, training, and mentoring (Mark Murphy, 2014). Unfortunately, the reality is that filing expense reports, signing off on purchase orders, and attending budget meetings often take over the bulk of your day. And while previous generations may have been okay with limited interactions with their manager — Millennials are different!

Millennials crave and respond to great positive coaching from managers. In a survey conducted by SuccessFactors, Millennials highlighted their number one source of development as their manager, but less than half (46%) of respondents felt that their managers actually delivered on this expectation (SAP SuccessFactors, 2014). Millennials aren't necessarily looking for managerial direction, but rather for help with their own personal development.

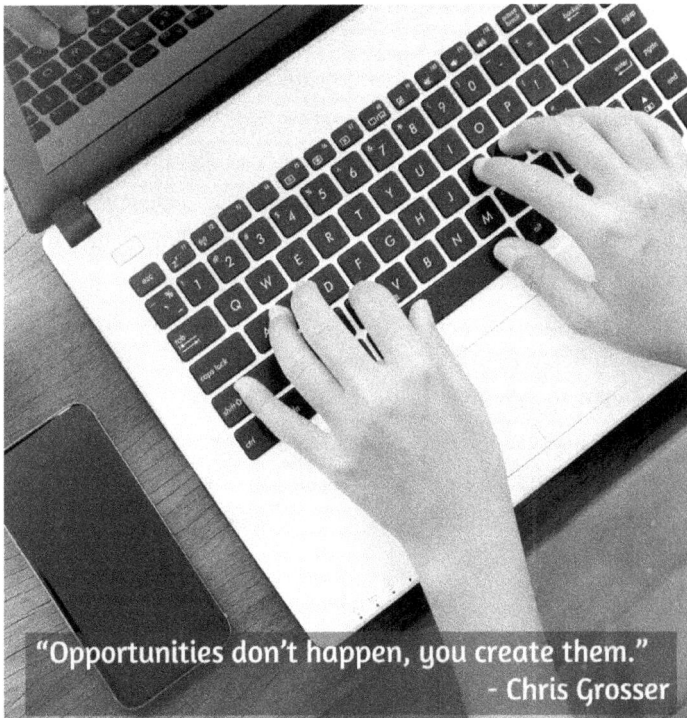

"Opportunities don't happen, you create them."
- Chris Grosser

Molly Missing Out

Molly has spent a decade and a half working her way up to where she is, managing five team members in the accounting department of a small cable company in the Midwest. She is 47 years old and began her career in accounts payable; now she is a team lead. For the last three years, she's enjoyed her new role as a manager. Brandon, one of her hires, is a recent graduate from an accounting program. With Brandon having only graduated not even a year prior, Molly placed Brandon as an entry-level accounts receivable clerk.

When he began, Molly committed to Brandon to meet with him for a weekly one-on-one meeting. But because of her daily duties and pressing matters, she cancelled on him most weeks. The result is that Brandon has only been able to meet with Molly about once a month so far, but she isn't overly concerned because she feels that Brandon is performing his job well. His reports are submitted on time each week and it does appear that he has quickly figured out the company's processes. Brandon seemed to be a good fit for the team during his first few months, but he hasn't assimilated as well to the organizational culture. Molly has begun to notice that Brandon doesn't seem to be as engaged in the team meetings as he was initially.

When he first started, he asked a lot of questions and even offered some great suggestions on how to streamline receivables processing, allowing the company to actually invoice faster. Molly's boss was really excited about this innovative idea, and her team was even recognized in the company's internal newsletter two months ago for such innovation.

Molly didn't get her usual response from Brandon when she sent him her usual quick email canceling, not rescheduling. Instead of his cordial reply of "okay, thanks," Brandon asked Molly if she could reschedule the meeting for a more convenient time because he really needed to talk. The soonest Molly could find an opening in her schedule was two days later. Brandon came to Molly's office for the meeting and handed her his letter of resignation. Needless to say, Molly was really flabbergasted!

So what went wrong? Brandon seemed like a great fit to the company; he caught on to the processes very quickly and even showed promising leadership skills early in his career with the company by presenting a great intrapreneurial idea. What's more, the company implemented it and recognized the whole team! Shouldn't Brandon be thrilled? Why isn't he then? Brandon, like most Millennials, has a strong desire to receive consistent feedback and coaching from his manager. The message Molly sent Brandon with the constant canceling of meetings is that Molly didn't respect or value Brandon.

Millennials don't leave companies — they leave their managers.

How do you ensure that you aren't like Molly, and that you don't allow valuable assets like Brandon to walk out your door?

Here's how you should move beyond just managing your Millennials and begin offering them opportunities to progress in their career within your company:

Tip #1: Be a great boss. Provide career-boosting training, development, and coaching to each of your team members. Help all team members capitalize on their strengths. Know who can play what role. Then you play, in many ways, the most critical role of understanding the career goals of your team members and working with each member to craft a plan to help them achieve their goals.

Tip #2: Widen the path. Don't let the company's preset career track be the only option open for your team members to advance. Be open to adjusting the plan to more closely match the interest, vision, and passion of your intrapreneurs.

Tip #3: Communicate talent development decisions. Provide information about when and how your company handles talent development, including succession planning, performance evaluation, and identification of high-potential talent. Hold frequent discussions with your intrapreneur to be sure that you are aware of his or her career vision and look for opportunities that support that growth.

Tip #4: Find the right challenge. To get work accomplished, managers tend to ask people to do things they already know how to do. This is particularly true in most companies today when managers are asked to do more with less and pre-existing proficiency is very helpful. But if you are not proactively thinking about special assignments or roles for team members with potential for advancement, then how will employees be able to continuously learn and grow? Help your team members hone in on their skills, behaviors, and actions so that they go on to take future assignments and opportunities. Having open conversations about where they want to go can help you identify what support, guidance, or training you can provide to help them work toward that goal.

Tip #5: Reshape the current job. Break the mold! Recast with custom specifications that fit your intrapreneur(s). Consider rotating tasks to give your intrapreneur the opportunity to take on a responsibility that would have normally gone to a more experienced team member. This gives the newcomer a shot to display their knowledge, and it gives the veteran employee a chance to step aside and give others the reigns. Provide opportunities to take on new challenges within the department. As you work to assign projects and tasks, give some thought to the unique duties you have as a manager. These are the skills that your employees may not be familiar with, but should be if they aim to move up within the organization. Then, find ways for your employees to start gaining experience in those areas.

Tip #6: Offer temporary assignments. Allow your team members to try out new roles within the company by joining a special project team or taking on a short-term role in other departments.

Tip #7: Allow for a struggle or two. When an employee needs help with a task, he or she typically comes to you, so you can either take over or provide the resource that will help accomplish the task. But when you're coaching your employees to help them progress in their career, it's more beneficial to push them to figure out how to get what they need on their own. For example, if an employee needs help with a financial spreadsheet, stop yourself from finishing it yourself and instead, introduce your employee to the head of the finance department and let them take it from there. It's not about demonstrating or delegating everything, it's about showing them how to use their resources. They don't have to know everything; they just need to know one thing that helps them learn everything — they need to know who to ask for what!

Tip #8: Make time. Schedule time to talk with your team member about his or her vision for development. Discuss the skills and behaviors that need to be learned or improved on and build out a plan to support this. Providing specific activities and goals encourages ongoing growth.

Tip #9: Establish networking opportunities. Organize or find professional networking opportunities. If your company doesn't currently offer employee resource groups, consider helping to get some started. These groups are great opportunities for team members to locate others with shared goals who can help support them as they grow within their career.

Tip #10: Create an ownership mentality. You can coach people day after day, but they won't feel secure enough to actually use new skills unless they feel like a trusted, valued, and impactful part of your company. Creating an ownership mentality begins with you trusting them and giving them authority to make certain decisions. When Millennials feel like an integral part of the company, it is much easier for them to begin to behave and contribute as intrapreneurs!

Activity — Growing from Within

Instructions: Evaluate the current career advancement opportunities for your team members. Use the following questions as a guide:

1. Are the strategic goals of your organization aligned to the career advancement opportunities you offer?

2. What differentiates your company's investment in your employees' career development from your competition?

3. What steps have you put in place to offer identifiable career paths for your intrapreneurs?

4. Identify the opportunities you have established for coaching and mentoring high-potential performers:

Keep in mind that Millennials are less likely to be interested in pay increases and more likely to be interested in learning new skills. They are less about the short-term monetary gains and more about the long-term future that comes from advancement. They are also more likely to value a career path than any other generation of workers within your organization. And finally, don't forget that they place a very high value on pathways to personal growth. The most effective way to ensure you do not lose this talent is to meet these needs head on.

Success Story — Progressing Internally

Keeping and motivating intrapreneurs requires a new way of looking at how we motivate and make sure the work is meaningful and challenging. Millennials are looking for forward progression in their career. Companies that have figured out how to embrace this desire in unique ways are having the biggest success in retaining these talented contributors!

Kimley-Horn is one such company. John Atz started with Kimley-Horn right after graduating from Clemson University with a civil engineering degree. He has been in a variety of roles within the company and now leads the company as president. Since 2009, John has served as the company president, displaying the spirit of career progression available with this engineering consulting firm.

> "One of the things that distinguishes us a bit is that we don't really have one career path. There is a lot of flexibility that we provide to people to follow the things that are of interest to them. A lot of organizations will be very hierarchical, very much 'you are at one step and then you move to the next and you move to the next.' Tenure plays a lot of role in your advancement and development and being given opportunities."

> "We tend to be much more focused on giving people the freedom to pursue the things that are of interest to them. If someone is performing well, we are willing to give them more rope and continue to allow them to grow at a pace

that's consistent with what they're comfortable with. I think we tend to see a lot of our younger staff gain experience at a very fast rate, particularly in our industry because I think we're a little freer in allowing them opportunities to explore the things that they have passions for."

Barry Barber, Director of Human Resources for Kimley-Horn, has also been with the company for some time and just celebrated his 21st anniversary with the company in 2015. Barry demonstrates why the type of individuals they hire make all the difference in their company's success:

"People that tend to do best with Kimley-Horn are those that are very proactive and really take the ball and run with it and also have a bent towards relationship building. Because the nature of consulting is that when our clients are buying our services, they're essentially buying our people. We need folks who are obviously very technically competent and very creative in their problem solving, but also have strong relationships."

"That's the type of people that we tend to seek out. It's also the type of people we tend to attract. That works out well. Once a person joins our firm, we try to have a good balance between on-the-job learning and training. The reality is that's where most folks have most of their development take place is just working side by side with more senior and experienced professionals. We believe that they have the opportunity to work with the very best in the industry when they come to Kimley-Horn, but we supplement that with a variety of training programs."

To listen to the entire interview with John Atz and Barry Barber, visit **The Millennial Career Playbook** website:

http://www.tmcpb.com/company-interviews/kimley-horn/

(Atz, Barber, 2015)

CHAPTER 6

Bending and Flexing

Millennials have grown up in a world where physical presence is optional: Shopping, banking, going to school, ordering food, and hanging out with friends have all transformed from physical activities to virtual opportunities from any device. This has created a presence that is just as strong, if not stronger than a physical imprint. Because they expect immediate satisfaction and accessibility, working virtually or desiring flexible time is natural. Millennials don't want to be measured by the hours they physically spend at a location, but rather by the output of what they produce.

Successful, growing companies attract and retain the best and brightest intrapreneurs by ensuring that flexibility is incorporated into the core of their company culture. This includes allowing opportunities for employees to set their own schedules as long as they get their work done. And, the payoff is not just for Millennials! These companies have found that Gen Xers and

Baby Boomers also care about this as well. Millennials, however, are leading the way in prioritizing job flexibility. In fact, many Millennials would actually give up pay or delay a promotion to achieve an ideal schedule (PriceWaterhouseCoopers, 2011).

Real Schedules for Real Employees

Alexandra is participating in a second-round interview for a position as an assistant project manager at Eaton Engineering. She is a senior at the local university with an impressive GPA of 4.0 and president of the student engineering group. She has completed two previous engineering internships with fairly large firms in other states over the course of her college experience. During the first-round interview she was ranked as the top candidate.

The interview is being conducted by Thomas, the HR manager, and Stephanie, the department head, with whom the hired candidate will begin to work. Both Thomas and Stephanie seem incredibly impressed with Alexandra. She comes to the interview very prepared. It is clear that she has researched the company and is well-aware of the current projects on which the company is working. Alexandra also has several innovative suggestions on how to work more efficiently to obtain subcontractor bids. Clearly, her academic background as well as her previous experiences as an intern have prepared her well to be a contributor right from the start!

As the interview is wrapping up, Thomas asks Alexandra if she has any additional questions. Alexandra says she does. She asks, "How much flexibility is there with the working hours for the position?" Thomas and Stephanie both look at each other, then at Alexandra. Finally, Stephanie asks, "Why do you ask?" Alexandra immediately responds, "I really need the freedom to take a short nap after lunch, this is when my energy is at its lowest point. I really work best late at night when my brain is most sharp!"

Thomas and Stephanie just stare at Alexandra. Then finally, Thomas replies, "Um, we don't really have a flexible schedule. We do expect our team to be in the office unless they are out in the field at a job site." Alexandra says, "Okay, thanks. I understand your position. I think that was my final question. Let me know if you need any additional information about my past experiences."

The next week, Thomas called Alexandra to offer her the position. He shared how excited he and the team at Eaton were at having her become one of the assistant project managers. Alexandra's response, "Thanks for the offer, but I will have to pass on this opportunity. I wish you and Stephanie well on your search."

Shocking, right? No, not really! Alexandra represents the 56.7% of Millennials who ranked flexibility and work location as one of the top three most important factors in an ideal work environment during a survey conducted by ttcInnovations (ttcInnovations, 2016).

Offering flexible work arrangements for your employees is not only a great way to attract intrapreneurs, it is also now the law in some locations, including Vermont and the city of San Francisco! So, be sure to check with your state or local labor department to ensure you are in compliance with current requirements.

Even if you are not obligated by law to accommodate job flexibility requests, you may be missing out on great potential intrapreneurs like Alexandra by not being open to the idea. How can you make flexibility work for your company? Below are five strategies that you might want to consider implementing:

Strategy #1: Not limiting vacations — Many companies now implement policies of unlimited or take-what-you-need vacations. Although at first, this sounds like it might create a massive opportunity for misuse, companies that have successfully implemented it have found that it really works well in helping to encourage a culture of mutual respect and trust. This policy works best in work environments with workloads that ebb and flow, where productivity and contribution are easily measured, and where employees have the freedom to structure their own time to ensure maximum productivity.

Strategy #2: Results-only work environment — The Results-Only Work Environment (ROWE) concept was developed by Cali Ressler and Jody Thompson (Thompson, 2010). In this strategy, team members are measured by performance, results, or output rather than by the hours they spend physically in the office or working on tasks. Creating a ROWE workplace enables flexibility for all types of employees within the company — those who need to attend daytime appointments, those looking to avoid heavy commute times, or those who are trading off family caregiving responsibilities with others. The most important factor in making this strategy work is consistently setting clear and measurable goals at mutually understood and agreed upon intervals of time. All team members must be aware of what they need to achieve and how their work contributes to the overall success of the organization.

Strategy #3: Working remotely — The ability to work remotely is definitely on the rise. According to a 2013 report from the U.S. Census Bureau, 13.4 million people worked at least one day at home per week, which is a 35% increase from the previous decade (U.S. Census Bureau, 2013). The rise in virtual communication is likely one of the biggest contributors to the success of this strategy. When setting up a remote workforce, communication, transparent dialogue, and access to information are essential.

Strategy #4: Timing work and working time — Your work team is likely increasingly made up of individuals who have evaluated their lifestyles and identified their unique productivity rhythms (employees like Alexandra from our story earlier). Commute times, family schedules, and other obligations factor into the ability of employees to get work done efficiently. Companies offering flexibility for when employees can put in their work time can retain the best and most loyal teams. The options for creating flexibility are limited only by the company's and the employees' imagination and successful implementation, but here are a few ideas:

- Compressed work week
- Flex hours
- Shift swaps
- Extra vacation or personal days
- Reduced daily designated office/field hours

Strategy #5: Job-sharing — One of the most common ways for specialized professionals to allow time needed to care for their personal needs is to partner with another professional to share one single job. Job-sharing is a great solution that enables two professionals to join together to offer a company combined experience and intelligence. The federal government has long promoted job-sharing within its own departments as an excellent opportunity to offer flexible work arrangements for those taking care of family, pursuing education, or seeking part-time work for other reasons.

Each type of flexibility offers its own set of benefits and challenges that you should discuss with your team when considering what you will put into place for your employees.

"We need to take a more flexible approach to both the workplace and the work we do; one that provides us both the physical and cognitive space to harness the incredible power, insight and experience we offer, but focused not on the individual processes but instead on the overall outcomes our organizations are seeking to achieve."
    – David Coplin

Activity — Implementing Flexibility

Instructions: Before sending any employees home to work or allowing a job-share, you need to first create a flexible-work strategy to determine what will be offered:

1. Identify departments that will be eligible for the program and describe why this new plan fits.

2. Identify the job roles that will be eligible for the program within each department.

3. Determine who will have the final say and duty to monitor any flex-work arrangements.

4. Decide on best metrics to be used to track productivity.

5. Determine an effective communication strategy to ensure clear expectations are shared.

Keep in mind that companies that don't appropriately plan for flexible-work strategies are generally the ones that claim flexible work makes their teams less productive. So plan for your success!

Success Story — Flexibility in Action

Companies that successfully implement flexible work options are reaping huge benefits such as cost savings, reduced turnover, and increased employee satisfaction. Ryan, a global tax firm with the largest indirect and property tax practices in North America, has been recognized by Fortune magazine as a "Best Place to Work" for Millennials, new college graduates, and women. Delta Emerson, President of the Global Shared Services unit at Ryan, shares how her company has reaped these benefits while attracting top talent after implementing flexibility with the launch of the *myRyan* program:

> "We have a unique, entrepreneurial approach to the way that we execute our business model. One of the draws we have is our very flexible work environment. Our team members can work anywhere, anytime, as long as they achieve the results we've mutually agreed upon. That's a little unique. *myRyan* has been in place for over eight years, and was designed in a way that doesn't cause people to have to raise their hands and ask permission. There's obviously a lot of communication, collaboration, and consideration."

Emerson explains the difference between the way many other companies attempt to implement a flexible work environment and *myRyan*:

"Many of the flex programs out there have boundaries and rules around them, forms to fill out, and individual employees are on record as being on flex or not. We really don't have those artificial boundaries in place. Our professionals are able to, on a daily, weekly basis, figure out where they need to be to get their jobs done. It sometimes depends on their work preference. Some like to be in an office setting working head-down. Others are more comfortable moving between remote locations than at an office. This kind of flexibility lets individuals lead their whole lives without guilt, i.e. go to a soccer game with a child, drop a child off at daycare, or take care of an elderly parent. None of those things are guilt factors anymore because employees are empowered to figure out where they need to be, and when they need to be there — including work — and getting the job done."

Implementing the *myRyan* program was a dramatic change for the company:

"When we first rolled out *myRyan* in 2008, it was a huge change because we had been perceived as, and actually were, a very draconian environment that put a huge emphasis on face time. So when our CEO, Brint Ryan, stood up in front of our management team in 2008 and said, 'We are going to do this,' — jaws dropped. He said, 'In exchange for incredible flexibility and freedom comes the responsibility and the accountability for producing results.' Then he went on to share what that would look like and what we were hoping for and expecting from our employees. His vision for *myRyan* was an environment where everyone focuses on results, not hours or face time. To do that, we had to make sure that we equipped people with the technology needed for them to have flexible work schedules and locations, including upgrading equipment so everybody in the company was on a level playing field."

"As he'll tell you himself, our CEO is a raging capitalist. He was invited to speak on Capitol Hill in February of 2012, along with Admiral Mike Mullen and the CEO of Deloitte, about why flexibility is important. He's very honest about the fact that he is in this to make money as a business and to make sure his company survives. To do that, he has to take care of people, and in order to take care of people, you have to honor their need to take care of every part of their lives. He recounted a story about himself, saying 'Even though I had been fighting this flexibility thing and I really appreciated the face time, I realized that in doing my own job, I have a flexible environment. Granted, being at the top of the organization, I could do that. But it dawned on me that if I can do this, everybody can do it.'"

"We soon realized that a flexible work environment had a positive ripple effect on every other metric that a CEO cares about. After implementing *myRyan*, our client satisfaction ratings were higher than ever, our revenue increased, turnover decreased, and our employee engagement scores were high. It quickly became apparent that a flexible work environment wasn't simply a great way to keep employees happy, but it was the smartest business move we've ever made."

"Brint Ryan would say that many of his partners, when we started down this path, just assumed this place was going to close its doors because nobody would show up. They thought our clients were going to wonder where we were and think we weren't being responsive. That didn't happen. Instead, quite the opposite. Our clients are happier than ever. People value *myRyan* so much that they will do anything to continue to work in an environment like this."

"The key to our success with this approach is two-fold: 1) We took great care to design the program, including developing training and guidelines for teams and managers, and 2) We created Key Performance Indicators (KPIs) and performance management tools to facilitate intelligent conversations about what constitutes success and results at individual and team levels."

"Ryan employees give more than 100% in a very self-disciplined way. It's a win-win for the company. It's a win-win for employees. It's a win-win for the children and the families of employees. It's not to say there aren't bumps in the road occasionally, but those can be resolved. It is definitely the right thing to do in this day and age because we're living in an environment and a world that allows us to be connected all the time. That can work for us. It can work against us. We believe that if used appropriately, technology, combined with flexibility and discipline, really enables a company like ours to succeed."

To listen to the entire interview with Delta Emerson, visit **The Millennial Career Playbook** website:

http://www.tmcpb.com/company-interviews/ryan/

(Emerson, 2015)

CHAPTER 7

Purposefully Driven

More than any previous generation, Millennials place an extreme importance on social causes and sense of purpose in their greater community. This sense of purpose is two-fold. The first is self-purpose; how do they fit into the organization? How is their work relevant? Does anyone care about what they contribute? The second is the purpose of the company; how does the company relate to the world at large? How does the company contribute? And, most importantly — does the company's concern with social responsibility match their own?

Six out of 10 Millennials within a focused study stated that a sense of purpose drives them toward selecting their current employer (Deloitte, 2016). And, while money is important to Millennials (they definitely do want competitive pay), what is more important is having a meaningful and fulfilling job. Millennials who derive meaning from their work are more than three times as likely to stay with a company! In fact, meaningful work is the highest single reason in a survey of more than 12,000 employees across a broad range of companies and industries (Porath, 2014) for why employees stay longer with a company. And as a bonus, employees who find meaning within their jobs don't just stay longer — they report 1.7 times higher job satisfaction and are 1.4 times more engaged at work! Clearly a win-win!

Losing Purpose

Jung was hired by a company to work in their corporate office as the Director of Training. He started work in October and was instantly impressed with the team of folks he met. On his first day, he was provided a list of people from different departments to meet with to learn about the company. At the end of that first day, the CEO invited him into the office to talk about Jung's first impressions and to hear a little about the company from the CEO's perspective. Jung felt like he had found a perfect match! Each of the people he spoke with shared that the number one priority for the company was to do the right thing for the customers. And, each department head shared some of the things their team did every day to live that philosophy.

Fast-forward three months: The entire team at corporate headquarters was brought together for a meeting. The chairman of the board led the meeting. He talked of how the company was entering into a new era, a new direction — a new FUTURE! And, to lead the company to this new future, he was excited to introduce the new CEO, Judith. He went on to say that the company was so lucky to have her join, as she had vast experience helping a variety of companies re-invent themselves to evolve with the changing economy.

Jung was interested and a bit puzzled; he hadn't heard any talk of the company taking a new direction or the past CEO leaving the company. But, he figured, maybe this was already in the works and since he was so new, he simply wasn't in the loop. As folks left the meeting, Jung overheard several people talking about the change. Many voiced serious concerns about it and one department head actually said that he had met people from Judith's last company and it was a complete disaster when she took over there!

Within two short months after the announcement, Jung could see that Judith had a lot of changes in store for the company. The first change was a complete overhaul of the company corporate office leadership. Within six months, the entire company had a new look and feel. Unfortunately, it wasn't just a logo change, it was a complete cultural change. Although the new leadership talked about how it was a fresh, new, innovative company, what Jung saw and heard was that the heart of the company was gone. Every meeting, every decision, and every focus appeared to be about how this company was going to increase revenue, increase locations, and dominate the field! What was gone was that central focus he found on his first day — how the company would do the right thing for every customer. Suddenly, it was all about the company. The size of the company, the revenue of the company — the LOOK of the company.

Jung no longer felt at home, and shortly after celebrating his one-year anniversary, he walked into the Vice President of Human Resources' office and handed in his resignation.

So what is the problem? The company culture! The company no longer focused on its customers and doing the right thing. The focus was now all about expansion and revenues. What started out as a great opportunity for Jung, a company that truly cared about doing the right thing, turned into the complete opposite. The company's central purpose changed and Jung felt it no longer matched what mattered most to him. The company sadly lost a great asset that day!

How can you ensure that you don't lose valuable team members like Jung? Here's how you and your company can be offering impactful and meaningful career opportunities:

Idea #1: Beginning with you — You must first know your own purpose and ensure that your company sees that purpose in you as a manager. It cannot be just the company that has a purpose — your own drive, passion, and energy should be at the forefront every single day.

Idea #2: Attaching work to ideals — Work becomes much more satisfying when the guiding principles reflect core values. The tone of the company's culture is set by the shared values you have in place. These values could include things such as:

- Being accountable
- Making a difference

- Focusing on details
- Keeping promises
- Meeting deadlines
- Helping others
- Being supportive to others
- Upholding company policies and practices
- Respecting others
- Demonstrating tolerance and acceptance

Idea #3: Recognizing meaningful moments — Purpose is not something that occurs continuously. It often happens in quick bursts throughout the span of a career. Take the time to really embrace these moments when they occur within your team members, as it will leave a lasting impression on the employee about how they view their job.

Idea #4: Building a relationship — Employees find meaning in their job when they are in contact with people who benefit directly from their work. Create time and opportunities for your team to share feedback from the people who benefit from the work they do each day. If their work supports your customers, give your team a way to connect to those customers. It can be as easy as sharing real testimonials, or even a visit to a location where customers can be met face to face. If your team's work is a directly benefits another department (internal customer), be sure to offer opportunities to connect with members from other departments.

Idea #5: Identifying why you do what you do — Team members need to have a clear understanding of how the work they are doing fits in with and supports the organization's values and purpose. They need to see that their work is helping the organization improve society in some way. Individuals experience their work as meaningful when it matters to others more than themselves.

Idea #6: Making your company more socially responsible — Avoid tokenistic corporate responsibility and instead commit to bold social goals. Integrate social change in all aspects of your operation. Here are just a few examples of meaningful social responsibility from some of today's most successful companies:

- **P&G's** Dawn products help volunteers with oil spill cleanups for animal and bird rescue.
- **The Walt Disney Company** focuses on reducing environmental impact of all its parks.
- **Starbucks** developed sustainable production of its coffee and has spearheaded campaigns that provide coffee trees to the farmers for every sale of coffee bean bags generated.
- **TOMS** donates a pair of shoes to a child in need for every pair of shoes sold.
- **Fairmont Hotel** cultivates honey beehives as part of its long history of environmental stewardship.
- **Walgreens** Get a Shot. Give a Shot® helps provide lifesaving vaccines to families in developing countries through the United Nations Foundation's Shot@Life campaign. Customers who get vaccinated help provide the same care to those who can't afford it for themselves.
- **Subaru** offers both intangible and tangible positive impact. They assure customers with their "lifetime

commitment to getting them home safely" in regard to teen drivers. Subaru also produces eco-friendly cars in green factories and their employees are not just encouraged, but expected to offer volunteer hours for various causes — animal shelters, children living in impoverished neighborhoods, and people who are sick or disabled.

Idea #7: Telling stories — Utilize your company's internal communications platforms (think newsletter or email profiles) to share some of the great examples of how the work your team does makes a difference. By sharing these stories, you remind your team of the important purpose each of you serve in your daily work.

"For, in the end, it is impossible to have a great life unless it is a meaningful life. And it is very difficult to have a meaningful life without meaningful work."
-James C Collins

Activity — Finding Purpose

Instructions: Use the following questions to have a frank and honest discussion with your team and create the potential for meaningfulness in your department:

1. Do your individual values match the company's values?

2. Do you feel appreciated?

3. Do you feel that your job tasks add value and are essential to the success of the work in which you are involved?

4. Do you feel that you are treated fairly?

5. How much control do you feel you have over the work you do?

6. Do you feel that you have opportunities to connect with others?

Asking these questions gives you an opportunity to begin a dialogue with your team. These questions can help uncover disconnections between what the company represents and what it actually does.

Success Story — Meaning in Action

Working in the restaurant industry can be really challenging. Popular culture is full of unflattering references and misconceptions about the employees' education, drive, and skillset. Despite the fact that one in 10 Americans currently works in a restaurant, one-third of Americans find their first job in a restaurant, and 50 percent of Americans work in a restaurant at some point in their working lives— restaurant work is still regarded with disdain. Many people may be surprised to learn that in 2015 Chili's ranked number 11 on Fortune's list of "100 Best Workplaces for Millennials" (Fortune, 2015). However, the employees at Chili's are not surprised by this at all! Chili's team members have extreme pride in all that they do each and every day.

The following story is just one example of how meaningful every customer interaction is to Chili's employees:

A 7-year-old named Arianna in Midvale, Utah ordered a cheeseburger and received it cut in half, because that's how burgers are served from the kids' menu at Chili's. The little girl wouldn't eat it, though, exclaiming, "It's broken!! I need another one that's fixed." With zero fuss, waitress Lauren Wells took it back, saying, "You know what, I'll have them cook you a new one!"

A few minutes later, manager Brad Cattermole came to the table, kneeled down, and said to Arianna, "I heard we gave you a broken cheeseburger! I am so sorry about that. We are

making you a brand new one that isn't broken, with pickles!"
When the replacement arrived, the little girl was overjoyed,
kissing the burger and saying, "Oh thank you!!! You fixed my
cheeseburger!!!" Arianna's older sister, Anna MacLean,
shared the entire incident on Facebook — with the explana-
tion that her little sister is autistic.

The story of the employees at that restaurant who went above
and beyond standard service resulted in nearly one million
online views, priceless positive publicity for Chili's, and a story
that demonstrates how each person within the organization has
the opportunity to contribute to their community in a truly
meaningful way!

To listen to the entire Chili's interview, visit **The Millennial
Career Playbook** website:

http://www.tmcpb.com/company-interviews/chilis/

(Chili's, 2015)

CHAPTER 8

Developing the Whole Person

M illennials don't just want to spend their time earning a paycheck; they want to invest time acquiring the skills and knowledge they need to grow both person- ally and professionally. This generation views work through an entirely different lens as compared to previous generations. They prioritize personal fulfillment and professional develop- ment (found rarely in the workplace anymore and widely var- ied at companies that do offer such opportunities) over cash bonuses and 401(k) programs (which are commodities that many companies do provide).

Learning philosophies have shifted; we now have a better un- derstanding of what's effective in learning and what isn't. We've really gotten to know our adult learners over the decades, and have grown in strides during the more recent years. However, lifelong learning is a continued commitment because our learners are still changing.

As more and more Millennials join organizations and even more move into leadership positions, we need to take a hard look at how prepared we are to provide for their needs — from new hire training to job-specific training and career development. Millennials have been adamant that they want different things out of their learning experiences, and you can be the one to provide the key opportunities that will help engage and retain them!

Finding a Future

Marlena recently quit her job. She had held the same position for two years and never once registered a complaint with her manager, so her resignation came as quite a shock! But it shouldn't have. The signs were there — the manager just missed them! The evening after turning in her letter of resignation, Marlena met up with a group of her college friends, most of whom were employed by companies in the area. When asked what she said to her manager, Marlena replied, "I said the working conditions were not conducive to effective performance. I couldn't really say the truth — that the training and professional development was awful!"

Marlena had actually worked in the training department — how ironic! For the entire two years, she tried to get her manager to consider making updates to the way training was developed and delivered. She even worked on her own without the help of her team to create a few sample micro-learning components that would demonstrate to her leadership just how easy it would be to update the current curriculum. She also tried to introduce the concept of mentorship with no avail.

Her manager felt that the current programs were perfectly fine. The materials provided employees with the information they needed to execute their jobs. In fact, in surveys of the training, the programs consistently scored well. What the manager didn't consider was that most of these programs had been developed with a completely different audience in mind. And the current audience — the surveyed participants — would be very unlikely to answer truthfully, just like Marlena, because of how the leadership ignored negative criticism. So the results of the survey were incredibly skewed.

Marlena had sat in on multiple new-hire classes and what she heard overwhelmingly from the participants was that they needed the opportunity to be out of the classroom and in the field working alongside someone who was currently doing the job they were starting. They wanted an opportunity to quickly learn the basics, apply that knowledge, and then move on to the next skill set. Job shadowing was their first priority, but it wasn't even being offered. This simply wasn't possible with the current six-week classroom new-hire program. And, the company leadership sided with the manager, failing to provide this sought after form of training.

So, what was her breaking point? Why did Marlena quit when she did? Marlena joined her local chapter of Association for Talent Development (ATD). After attending several local events, Marlena recognized that her company culture was not ready for Millennials. The leadership as a whole lacked a shared understanding that this newest generation in the workforce has a dramatically different approach to learning and development. While attending these chapter meetings, Marlena realized that her current company was in fact the minority, and the majority of the companies participating in this personal development organization shared her passion for adapting the learning culture to meet the evolving needs of the employees.

During the most recent meeting, she met the Director of Mentoring at a local participating company. This gentleman was so excited about helping his company grow leaders from the inside! Marlena decided right then and there that she couldn't continue working with a company that didn't share her passion for helping employees learn and grow in meaningful ways. Although she didn't have a new job lined up yet, she resolved that she would be okay because she could find a new position, confident in the fact that there were several local companies out there looking for intrapreneurs! She couldn't wait to join a new company and continue the revolution to help revitalize and instill conducive learning environments!

Is Marlena unique in her response to her company's training offering? Sadly, NO! Remember the statistic from the introduction chapter — only 16% of Millennials working in companies see themselves continuing with their current employer within the next few years. And the turnover rates are even more challenging within the earliest years of employment. In fact, 60% of all Millennials exit their companies in less than three years after being hired (Grovo, 2016). The cost of this turnover is staggering: 87% of companies that participated in the Grovo study report between $15,000 and $25,000 in cost for each Millennial employee they have to replace. And, not only do you risk losing the individual employee, but imagine the larger cost to your company in lost opportunities for new ideas, processes, products, and innovation when the Millennial that leaves is an intrapreneur? The cost of that loss may be way more than your company can bear.

Is the future hopeless? Absolutely not! You can make an immediate impact to alter these statistics by embracing and supporting Millennials' (especially intrapreneurs') strong desire for development. Following the suggestions below can help ensure you are offering engaging content and development experiences that focus on what your intrapreneurs really care about:

Tip #1: Onboard with intention. Millennials put a premium on doing work that truly matters. During your onboarding of new team members, don't just drop a company handbook filled with policies and procedures on their desk. And, *please*, don't plug them into antiquated e-learning modules about rules and regulations! Instead, invest your time, resources, and training dollars to educate new employees extensively about your company's goals and visions. Share the history, but do it in a way that connects and resonates with a generation that has grown up with technology! Be sure that at the conclusion of onboarding, your new team members know where you and your company are looking to go and that they can help you get there in a meaningful and challenging way.

Tip #2: Get specific. A key characteristic that intrapreneurs share is an internal goal to advance their individual skills. Demonstrate to your team members that you understand and support this desire to become better performers by creating developmental opportunities that are customized to their role within the company and helping them evolve within their role. Don't just deliver blanket companywide training content.

Tip #3: Go mobile. Too many companies are still offering training on clunky, disjointed systems that are inconvenient to access. Millennials have literally grown up alongside technological advancements. They are well aware of the opportunities out there and are 100% comfortable using their mobile device as a learning portal. If your training isn't available whenever and wherever your team wants to access it, it may as well not exist.

Tip #4: Create engaging content. Speaking of technology — not only is the ability to access training content from anywhere at any time important — the content must be high quality and extremely engaging. Keep in mind that your content is competing against the ever-advancing technologies found on the internet. If your content is boring, dated, or poorly executed, you will quickly lose your Millennial audience. Companies that require employees to sit through training that does not resonate send a strong message — this company is not RELEVENT! The last thing an intrapreneur wants to do is stay within a company that offers outdated, boring, and last century training! You are basically advertising to the Millennials that innovation and intrapreneurialism is not welcome within the organization.

Tip #5: Learn by doing. The ability to apply recently acquired knowledge instantly is important to Millennials. In an era where you can quickly go to YouTube® to view a video on how to do just about anything, Millennials need the same approach to learning content. Build practice activities and meaningful performance-based assessments into your training content. This gives Millennials the instant context and feedback they crave. As an added bonus, this dramatically increases the likelihood that they'll actually retain and apply what they have just learned. Win-win!

> "Tell me and I forget.
>
> Teach me and I remember.
>
> Involve me and I learn."
>
> – Benjamin Franklin

Tip #6: Weave development into everyday work. Old-school learning where a facilitator serves as basically a talking head ad nauseam is not likely to inspire your intrapreneur to innovate, much less remain at your company! Find creative, cutting edge solutions to deliver just-in-time content to your team. Consider using a micro-learning-based approach to deliver quick hits of content in engaging ways. Invest in a great performance support solution that allows your team to access solutions at the moment of need.

Tip #7: Facilitate informal sharing opportunities. Create an environment that supports informal get-togethers where employees can hang out at lunch or after hours with each other to talk about what they are working on or problems they are solving. Give employees an opportunity to share knowledge across teams and departments. Who knows, a great solution may come from a fellow employee two floors down!

Tip #8: Create effective mentoring programs. Mentorship is one of the most desired types of development according to a survey of 527 Millennial professionals (Virtuali, 2014).

Not only is it much desired, it is also one of best ways to increase productivity. While training on its own has shown a 22.8% increase in employee productivity — when coupled with mentoring, that number rises to 90%! New employees who have mentors acclimate to an organization twice as quickly as those who don't have a mentor. What's even more impressive — employees who take part in a mentoring program have a 25% higher retention rate than those who do not participate (Mutual Force, 2015).

The idea behind mentorship is quite simple; create a mutually beneficial relationship in which both the mentor and the mentee participate and contribute to one another's goals and expectations — a relationship that is open to change and demonstrates a willingness to learn. To develop a successful mentorship program for your company, you'll need:

- Communication: Make sure that everyone in your company is aware that mentoring is going on and is supported by management. Senior executives within the company need to be on board with the mentoring program and be a part of the communication. By having management serve as mentors, everyone in the company knows that it is important and of value.

- A mentoring culture: Mentoring isn't a single day event — it is a culture. A mentoring culture continuously focuses on building the mentoring capacity, competence, and capability of the organization.

- Multiple mentors: Millennials in general do not have or want a single mentor — they desire an open environment to explore and connect with any number of people who have the knowledge, experience, and wisdom they seek. Remove the barriers or expectations of single mentor/mentee partnerships.

- Technology to increase connections: To expand the mentoring experience and create a truly open environment, you may need to incorporate technology. Mentoring doesn't always have to be face to face; it could involve a mixture of virtual and traditional in-person mentoring. This opens the door for Millennials to forge new relationships outside of the traditional boundaries of the office environment.

- Participation: Encourage everyone to serve in a mentor role if possible. Some use the term "reverse mentoring," but honestly, it is all about mentoring. It is not reverse mentoring if the Millennial is serving as the mentor; it is simply a person with the expertise sharing knowledge with another person who has not yet obtained that skill.

Tip #9: Say goodbye to traditional training. A side-by-side comparison survey of learning preferences (ttcInnovations, 2016) between Millennials and managers found that while Millennials said they like to learn best from peers, mentors, or their own independent research, managers thought that Millennials preferred to learn in self-paced online courses, virtual classes, and webinars.

Millennials overwhelmingly responded in a panel interview that they learned best from hands-on experiences. Does this mean that we should get rid of traditional learning? No, not at all. But you do need to assess your current offerings to see if they are still practical for the emerging workforce:

- Instructor-led training: This is definitely a great option for Millennial training — however, you need to be sure that the training is engaging, relevant, and immediately applicable. This actually has great potential because it provides the opportunity for face-to-face communication and collaboration, as well as immediate feedback.

- Virtual instructor-led training: This is a dynamic learning option for organizations with a dispersed population and a need to train at minimal cost. A high level of engagement is critical. Good training engages the learner — we all know this. Engaging someone who has grown up texting while listening to music and checking email all at the same time takes extra effort. Virtual learning cannot be a talking head, and it especially cannot be a talking head who rests on the same PPT slide for 10 consecutive minutes.

- Online training: This is also a wonderful option for a dispersed population. Learners can go at their own pace and consume at a rate that is appropriate for them. But, contrary to popular belief, just because a course is online does not mean it is Millennial-friendly. Boring online training is just as bad as monotone, talking head instructor-led training — maybe even worse, as it doesn't even have the benefit of human connection that an instructor provides.

Activity — How Millennial-Ready is Your Learning and Development?

Instructions: Complete the grid below by identifying one of your current development programs that you feel needs to change to help you retain the intrapreneurs on your team.

Description of the strategy or program:	Who is responsible for the program (for example, executive level, manager, HR, or training dept.)?
Description of what needs to change:	Which individuals or departments need to be involved to make the change?

Examples of what it should look like or accomplish after the change is implemented:	Level of effort / time frame needed to make the change:
Small steps you can take to begin now:	Type of support needed (for example; financial, leadership buy-in, policy change and so on):

Repeat this process to evaluate additional programs or strategies that need to be changed to create more effective development opportunities throughout your organization. Imagine how making these changes will change the future of not only your department but your entire company!

Success Story — Developing by Mentoring

Mentoring programs offer a development tool that is especially attractive to Millennials. They provide opportunities for frequent feedback and maximize relationships. There is also a great side benefit in that it is a very cost-effective development strategy requiring very little in the way of external resources.

Edward Jones is an example of a company that has established an incredibly successful mentorship program. Penny Pennington, Principal – Client Strategies Group, explains, "Mentorship is one of the linchpins of our culture." Edward Jones has a very successful formal training program, but mentorship occurs both formally and informally at the firm:

> "The way that we think about developing our careers is what we call a 70/20/10 model. We believe that seventy percent of our growth and development professionally happens on the job. It comes from the work that we're doing. Twenty percent happens as a result of people watching the work that we're doing, observing us and giving us good, candid feedback. Then ten percent of our development comes from more formal courses, reading, and learning. Many people think that most development comes more from the formal courses. Instead, we gain the most experience and confidence through the work that we do every day."

Penny continues by sharing how their balance is a formula for success:

> "When we think about rapidly developing high potential folks, we think critically as leaders about every individual's 70/20/10. We think about the work they're decked against, not just to get that work done but to ensure that they're growing their capability. Then, as their leaders, give them feedback about what they're seeing, what's going really well and things they might consider next time they have similar projects. We know that development can be even more rapid."

This strong commitment to professional development and the mentorship program is working well for Edward Jones. The company has appeared 17 times on Fortune's list of "100 Best Companies to Work For" and ranked in the top ten thirteen times. They have also been recognized by Wealth Management Magazine as the best place for financial advisors to work based upon feedback from financial advisors themselves.

To listen to the entire interview with Penny Pennington, visit **The Millennial Career Playbook** website:

http://www.tmcpb.com/company-interviews/edward-jones/

(Pennington, 2016)

CHAPTER 9

Innovating the Future

Innovation is truly the heart and soul of the intrapreneur — and companies that harness this spirit are the future! Companies with a formalized innovation strategy grew eight percent faster than other companies in terms of revenue. Intrapreneurs want to create and they want to be recognized for their ideas. The companies willing to support these initiatives are going to have the most success (Deloitte, 2016).

Millennials in general view innovation as the key purpose of business and just as important as profit. This is a real shift in business dynamics. Just take a look at some of these key findings that underscore this embracing of innovation from the Deloitte Millennial Survey:

- 78% of Millennials feel innovation is essential for business growth.
- 71% believe innovation in business improves society.

- 66% say innovation is critical when selecting a potential employer.
- 62% describe themselves as innovative.

Ideas into Reality

Innovation is the process of translating an idea into a product or service that creates value and generates revenue. Innovation does come with inherent risks — that revolutionary idea may take months, even years, to develop. Even then, it may end up on a back shelf because consumers have no interest once it appears in the marketplace. However, without innovation, companies are likely to find that they are a dying breed while their competitors jump forward in the market.

3M is a great example of a company that has continuously stayed on top, powered by a culture of innovation. The story of the creation of Post-it® Notes by 3M demonstrates how a culture of innovation encouraged intrapreneurs with a vision to create something awesome! In 1968, Spencer Silver was working on creating a super strong adhesive for use in the aerospace industry. However, one formula created by Silver yielded a rather weak pressure-sensitive adhesive agent called Acrylate Co-polymer Microspheres.

While this adhesive didn't provide the strong adhesive properties which were then of initial interest, it did have two unique properties. The first was that when the adhesive was applied to a surface, it could be peeled away without leaving any sticky residue. The second was that the adhesive was reusable. But, even with these two unique properties, neither Silver nor any other team member at 3M then envisioned a marketable product employing these properties to meet customers' needs, so the adhesive took a back seat to other innovations for a time.

Fast forward a few years: Geoff Nicholson enters the picture as the Products Laboratory Manager. Silver hadn't given up trying to find ways to use his adhesive, and he approached Nicholson with a new idea for its use. Silver felt that the adhesive could be applied to a bulletin board, making a sticky surface so papers could be attached without the need of tacks or tape. The paper could then be removed from the board, leaving no residue on the back. This idea brought the original innovation back into development and an adhesive bulletin board was launched. While this was a great use for the adhesive, the innovation didn't stop with the bulletin board.

Months later, Art Fry, a Product Development Engineer for 3M, learned about the adhesive from a colleague who had attended one of Silver's seminars discussing the low-tack adhesive. Fry also sang in his church choir. It was a challenge he faced during singing that led to the next innovation with the adhesive. The problem he had was that his song page markers kept falling out of the songbook while singing. He had the idea that perhaps the adhesive could be used to adhere slips of paper temporarily in his hymnal. Fry approached Nicholson and Silver with the suggestion to put the adhesive on small pieces of paper so they could stick to any smooth surface — but also be removed without leaving residue or harming the surface.

It took more development work to implement industrial production and bring this innovation to the consumer, but several months later, test sales began for what were then known as "Press 'n Peel Pads". There wasn't a huge market immediately, but the intrapreneurs at 3M did not give up on the product. Free samples were given away in a handful of test markets, including one in Boise, Idaho that targeted administrative assistants and office workers. The reorder rate from people who had received free samples skyrocketed. Around the same time, the pads were reintroduced commercially under the "Post-it" brand, a brand 3M was already using on other products featuring the unique adhesive. By the early '80s, the company had released "Post-it® Notes" broadly throughout the United States and internationally, where they became a huge success.

So, although the initial formulation and application of this idea took a few years, the innovation is now known worldwide. Even with the rise of digital tools, Post-it® Notes remain a mainstay in offices around the world.

Imagine how different 3M and the world would be today if Spencer Silver and Art Fry hadn't held true to their intrapreneurial spirit and pushed forward with their vision of innovation!

Unfortunately, not all intrapreneurs will stay with a company when their desires to be innovative are shot down. These innovators are seeking out a workplace that will encourage them to unleash their creative ideas. If you are looking to attract and retain this generation, think about ways that you can adapt your culture to create an environment that will allow them to fulfill their desire to innovate.

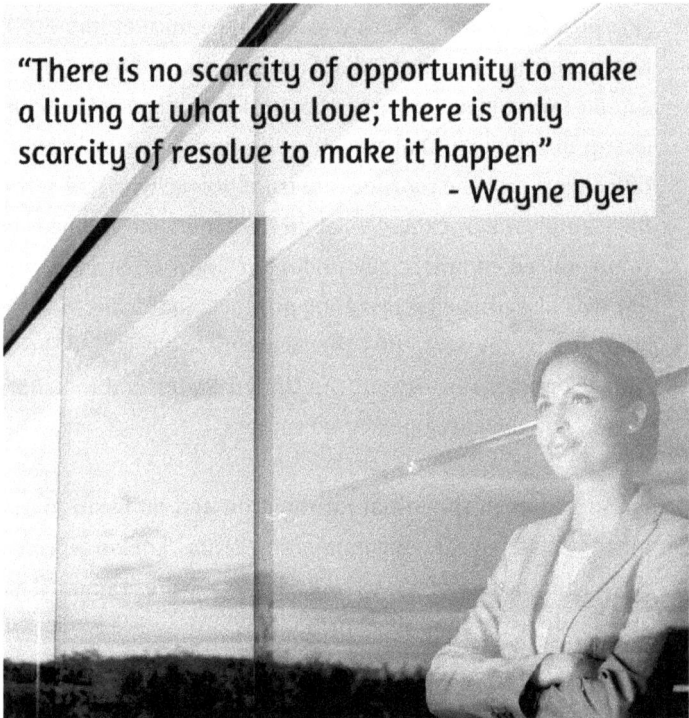

> "There is no scarcity of opportunity to make a living at what you love; there is only scarcity of resolve to make it happen"
> — Wayne Dyer

Here are some strategies to help you get started creating an environment that promotes innovation:

Strategy #1: Create innovative intent. Evaluate your company mission. Make sure it reflects a vision that welcomes innovation. A company mission statement that reads something like, "Become the #1 internet provider" doesn't offer any guidance to employees on how to get there. To create an innovative environment, ensure your mission statement details the manner in which you want to change the world. Take that original mission statement and reframe it: "To improve our customers' connection with the world by offering state-of-the-art technology." This new mission statement makes it abundantly clear that the goal of the company is to search out innovation!

Strategy #2: Build an inspiring workspace. Imagine sitting inside a three-foot by two-foot taupe fabric-covered cubicle under a series of florescent tube lights listening to the hum of 30 co-workers' voices...feeling inspired yet? Probably NOT! Now, picture yourself and your team working in a large open space with cozy little nooks filled with comfortable conversation pieces scattered around, large windows with sunlight pouring in, and a kitchenette in the corner stocked with healthy (okay — and not-so-healthy) snack options. Large whiteboards and markers scattered around the room. Awesome state-of-the-art technology products available on-demand...now how is your inspiration level? Likely much higher! Even if you don't have the ability to build your office environment from scratch — work with your team to identify ways to make your workspace a starting point to encourage an outpouring of creative juices.

Strategy #3: Form a diverse team. Unless you are in the business of cloning, selecting a team filled with people who think, believe, and create just like you do will be a sure way to fail. If you want to encourage innovation, you have to select a diverse team whose strength lies in its members' wide range of experiences, education, and cultural backgrounds to build off of each other.

Strategy #4: Schedule unstructured time. One of the biggest challenges managers face is finding time. Often the urgent needs overtake the important needs. Running around stomping out fires and chasing short-term targets keeps you from thinking and planning for the future. Finding time to give intrapreneurs the ability to innovate is tough! However, just think about the cost of NOT innovating. Can you really afford that? Consider scheduling a pocket of time that is designated as "free time" to experiment with new ideas. Google offers their employees 10% free time for innovation. Atlassian offers employees "FedEx Days" — paid days off to work on any problem they want; but there is a catch — they have to deliver something of value 24 hours later. Apple offers Blue Sky, which allows some workers to spend a few weeks on pet projects. Intuit goes even further; they offer their best innovators three months of unstructured time to be used either all at once or spread out over six months for part-time exploration of new opportunities.

Strategy #5: Encourage side-intrapreneurism. MTV recently surveyed Millennials and found that 78% believe it is important to have a side project at work that could potentially lead to a different career (MTV, 2015). Offering intrapreneurs the opportunity to do a side project unrelated to their core job is a great way to encourage innovation while keeping the employee invested in your company.

Strategy #6: Host a hackathon. Even if you aren't a software company, you can create an event to encourage intrapreneurs to pitch innovations to a panel of judges. Offer the winners funding, space, and most importantly, time to take the idea from concept to reality. Your company retains ownership and the intrapreneur receives all the support necessary to build out the idea. Win-win!

Strategy #7: Reward risk taking. If you continue doing what you are currently doing as a company, likely your company will quickly lose relevancy. Reward your intrapreneurs for taking risks that are counter to the current status quo. If you want to ensure that your company continues to grow and remain relevant in the marketplace, you must have team members who are creating their own disruption by opening the door for innovation.

Strategy #8: Fashion a group think tank. Pull together people with entirely different skill sets and perspectives to work on a big project. Approaching a problem from different perspectives can bring unexpected breakthroughs in thinking and result in amazing innovations.

Strategy #9: Measure what matters. Often, it isn't coming up with ideas that's the problem. The challenge is turning them into something real that delivers an impact. How do you determine what metrics to use to measure that impact? Customer-oriented numbers are important. For example, Facebook set instances of users returning to the site as an early measurement to determine success and all their focus was on blowing out this single metric. However, customer focus isn't the only way to drive innovation. Proctor & Gamble realized the importance of outside partnerships in driving market share. Therefore, they decided to measure and increase the percentage of new products that used technologies from partners. The outcome of this was that innovation jumped from 10% to more than 50%, which resulted in new products including Mr. Clean Magic Erasers® and Tide Pods®. Imagine not having those handy household helpers!

Activity — Innovation Inventory

Instructions: Use the following survey to evaluate your readiness to innovate.

Question	Always	Often	Rarely	Never
Do you communicate an exciting vision for the work your company pursues?				
Do you demonstrate sustained, visible support for the projects you have approved?				
Does your team remain highly engaged in their work on important business opportunities even when faced with challenges?				
Are team members inspired to challenge the status quo?				
Do team members communicate frequently?				
Do you make team members openly share opinions and ideas?				
Do your team members make an				

effort to under-stand different per-spectives?				
Do your team members build on and adapt each other's ideas?				
Are groups are set up with cross-func-tional representa-tion to pursue new ideas?				
Do you empower team members to do what it takes to accomplish goals?				
Are groups pursu-ing new ideas that are important to the business reor-ganize themselves to respond to changing condi-tions and insights?				
Do you make it safe to fail?				

Effective innovation requires constant energy, creative fric-tion, flexible structures, and purposeful discovery. If you answered "rarely" or "never" to any question, use this as an opportunity to seek out help to work on that area of inno-vation. Take note of where you are faltering, use it as fuel for your drive. And refer back to this exercise as your team and you become more innovative

Success Story — Nurturing Innovation

Innovation is essential to the growth of your company. Creating a culture that is both fluid and creative will help you attract the intrapreneurs who will deliver that innovation.

No matter the size of your company, your industry, or your budget, if your company has a culture that supports innovation, you will succeed. 3M is a great example of how company culture has consistently set the tone for great innovation.

Fortune Magazine Journalist Marc Gunther explains how 3M is the gold standard in innovation (Gunther, 2010):

> "3M is not a conglomerate like GE or United Technologies, which own a variety of industrial businesses that operate, for the most part, on their own. Nor, like Apple or Sony, is it a technology company that focuses on a single industry or two, i.e., consumer electronics and entertainment. Instead, 3M — a supplier to all of those companies — is a set of businesses organized around a big, busy, and intellectually productive R&D lab, which researches new technologies and processes, and then develops them into products. The company's purpose, as best as I can tell, is to invent useful new things. Its unique competitive advantage is a culture that fosters innovation."

3M's VP of Global HR Business Operations Jon Ruppel shares what upholds their renowned recognition as experts in innovation:

> "We have a well-established reputation for innovation. It is the backbone of our company. Our Vision is: 3M technology advancing every company, 3M products enhancing every home, 3M innovation improving every life. One example I'd like to share with you spans back approximately 90 years ago and exemplifies many aspects of our culture. In the early 1920s, we had an employee named Dick Drew who had the job of testing waterproof sandpaper products at body paint shops. During his visits to the body shops, he would hear complaints about creating two-toned lines on cars, a fad that was just coming into fashion. At the time, body shops used a sticky mess of adhesives, paper, and spray paint to create the look, but often the glue stuck too tightly and had to be scraped off, which ruined the paint finish."

> "He brought back what he heard and became committed to figuring out how he could help create a solution. He started working with a 3M scientist to use the sticky backing of sandpaper and created what we now know today as Scotch™ masking tape. The reason why I bring this up is that it wasn't Drew's job, but our culture of innovation and the freedom that we allow our people to create these types of moments and actions spawns this kind of innovation."

Ruppel explains that being intentional in scheduling time to innovate is key, but allowing innovation to be somewhat organic should also be a focus of management:

> "This type of thinking is now codified in 3M as our 15 percent culture, which originated from stories like Dick Drew's. Our 15 percent culture encourages 3Mers to spend 15 percent of their time exploring their own innovative ideas and solutions. Collaboration is key for an innovative company. We have a large population of employees, but we emphasize that you're only a couple phone calls or emails away from someone who can help answer your question. We offer different ways to collaborate. For example, most of my direct reports on my Human Resources team don't even live in our St. Paul, Minn. headquarters. We work together across the world through virtual technology. It's a structure that is instantaneous and collaborative, and it's what supports our culture of innovation."

> "Combining our company's Vision, our 15 percent culture, collaboration, and our global reach and mindset makes for a strong, positive corporate culture. It's what we call internally, 'experimental doodling.' One of our most famous CEOs, William McKnight, is often quoted as saying, 'If you put fences around people, you get sheep. If you give people the room they need, they innovate.' Intellectual freedom is something we hold near and dear in our culture. Listening to everyone who shares their idea, no matter how initially absurd it may sound, could help bring about an important breakthrough or new invention."

To listen to the entire interview with Jon Ruppel, visit **The Millennial Career Playbook** website:

http://www.tmcpb.com/company-interviews/3m/

(Ruppel, 2016)

Final Thoughts

I ntrapreneurs are key drivers of the growth and success of your organization. Creating a culture that promotes this spirit of intrapreneurship starts with you. Attracting and retaining intrapreneurs assures that you will have the talent necessary to drive progress, solve complex problems and bring a passion to your organization.

Recognizing and supporting intrapreneurs on your team will make you better equipped to cultivate a space for them to grow and succeed, while ensuring your department and your company in its entirety thrives. Championing intrapreneurship is without a doubt the best way to safeguard your organization against becoming irrelevant and to successfully innovate now and into the future.

When you empower your team to be inventive by outfitting them with the tools, time, resources, and support necessary, you benefit by having team members with greater commitment, ownership, and ultimately products and services with greater quality and marketability to bring to the marketplace.

You as the manager have an important role in being the one who unleashes the intrapreneurs on your team, attracts additional intrapreneurs, and ultimately retains a strong, steadfast team!

Activity — Making a Commitment to Your Team

Instructions: Take a few minutes to help your team unleash their intrapreneurial spirit by creating a list of affirmatives you will commit to achieving.

Timeline	Commitment
3 weeks from now, I will….	
3 months from now, I will…	
3 years from now, I will…	

By documenting your commitment, you are one step closer to becoming a leader who is able to help your team achieve their goals. Hold yourself accountable for these commitments by sharing them with someone else.

Three weeks from now, read back through the book and complete the exercises again, reflecting on your initial answers and the progress you have made. Then offer the counterpart to this guide, *Unleashing the Intrapreneur: Changing The Face of Corporate America One Millennial at a Time*, to your team to aid in their development as intrapreneurs.

Three months from now, complete the exercises with your team and ask them to objectively share whether or not you as a manager are upholding these practices and whether or not they've followed your guidance (and that of their guide, *Unleashing the Intrapreneur*)

Three years from now check the progress of the team and see if the team is where you envisioned you'd be. If you've followed this guide, and supported your team, then you and the company will be right where you should be – trusting in and transitioning to the leadership of the most successful intrapreneurs, the Millennial generation.

"It's not just about seeing the connections and opportunities, it is also the act of weaving possibilities together to create something new and exciting."

– Dylan Sherlock

Mentions

Atz, J. and Barber, B. (2015). Kimley-Horn. (D. a. Wooldridge, Interviewer)

Chili's. (2015). (D. a. Wooldridge, Interviewer)

Debbie Wooldridge and Hy Bender. (2016). *The Milliennial Career Playbook*. Retrieved from TMCPB: http://www.tmcpb.com/

Deloitte. (2016). *The 2016 Deloitte Millennial Survey Winning over the next generation of leaders*. Retrieved from https://www2.deloitte.com/content/dam/Deloitte/global/Documents/About-Deloitte/gx-millenial-survey-2016-exec-summary.pdf

Dole, L. (2015). Tumblr. (D. a. Wooldridge, Interviewer)

Donovan, A. (2015). PWC. (D. a. Wooldridge, Interviewer)

Emerson, D. (2015). Ryan. (D. a. Wooldridge, Interviewer)

Fortune. (2015). *100 Best Workplaces for Millennials*. Retrieved from http://fortune.com/best-workplaces-millennials/2015/

Fortune Magazine. (2016). *100 Best Workplaces for Millennials*. Retrieved from Fortune: http://fortune.com/best-workplaces-millennials/

Gentry, L. L. (2015). Ultimate Software. (D. a. Wooldridge, Interviewer)

Grovo. (2016). *The Disappearing Act: Why Millennials Leave Companies - and How L&D Can Entice Them To Stay.*

Gunther, M. (2010, September 27). *Why 3M is Unique.* Retrieved from The Energy Collective: http://www.theenergycollective.com/marcgunther/44153/why-3m-unique

Mark Murphy, F. &. (2014). *Optimal Hours with the Boss' Study North America Research Overview.*

Mental Health Foundation. (2016). *Work-life balance.* Retrieved from Mental Health Foundation: https://www.mentalhealth.org.uk/a-to-z/w/work-life-balance

Merriam-Webster. (n.d.). *Communication.* Retrieved from Merriam-Webster: http://www.merriam-webster.com/dictionary/communication?utm_campaign=sd&utm_medium=serp&utm_source=jsonld

Millennial Branding. (2012). *American Express Study.* Retrieved from Millennial Branding Navigating You To Future Success: http://millennialbranding.com/american-express-study/

Mutual Force. (2015, January 11). *Mutual Force.* Retrieved from Top 26 benefits or real examples of workplace mentoring program: http://www.slideshare.net/mutualforce/top-26-benefitsofworkplacementoringprogram

Pennington, P. (2016). Edward Jones. (H. Bender, Interviewer)

PriceWaterhouseCoopers. (2011). *Millennials at Work.* Retrieved from pwc: https://www.pwc.com/m1/en/services/consulting/documents/millennials-at-work.pdf

PwC. (2013). *Hr Management Services*. Retrieved from
 pwc.com: http://www.pwc.com/gx/en/hr-
 management-services/pdf/pwc-nextgen-study-
 2013.pdf

Ruppel, J. (2016). 3M. (D. a. Wooldridge, Interviewer)

SAP SuccessFactors. (2014). *Oxford Exconomics' Workforce
 2020 Research.*

Skift. (2017, January). *Travel Habits of Americans: 34% of
 Americans Didn't Take a Break in 2016* Retrieved
 from https://skift.com/2017/01/30/travel-habits-of-
 americans-34-of-americans-didnt-take-a-break-in-
 2016/

Thompson, C. R. (2010). *Why Work Sucks and How to Fix It:
 The Results-Only Revolution.* Portfolio.

ttcInnovations. (2016). *Millennial Generation Survey.*

U.S. Census Bureau. (2013). *United States Census Bureau How
 Do We Know*. Retrieved from United States Census
 Bureau:
 http://www.census.gov/hhes/commuting/files/2012
 /Home-
 based%20Workers%20in%20the%20United%20Stat
 es%20Infographic.pdf

Virtuali. (2014). *Engaging Millennials through Leadership
 Development.*

Index

ABOUT THE AUTHOR

Debbie Wooldridge, founding president and CEO of DW Training and Development, Inc. dba ttcInnovations, had an idea for helping businesses improve their performance through effective training strategies and programs.

Under her skillful and experienced leadership, ttcInnovations provides businesses with engaging learning solutions that adopt a host of performance support options. Through instructor-led and web-based training programs utilizing system simulations, virtual environments, and other innovative approaches, Debbie's company has ultimately helped businesses enhance on-the-job performance, improve their customers' satisfaction, deliver significant business results, and achieve their goals. Debbie's company has also created The Millennial Project, an interactive two-day workshop that provides companies with the tools and strategic roadmap needed to improve workforce processes and productivity.

Debbie is also the author of, *Unleashing the Intrapreneur – Changing the Face of Corporate America One Millennial at a Time*

www.ingramcontent.com/pod-product-compliance
Lightning Source LLC
Chambersburg PA
CBHW060318220326
41598CB00027B/4361